W9-ABL-043

R. L. STEVENSON

J S Sargent R A pinxt

Yours truly

Robert Louis Stevenson

R. L. STEVENSON

A CRITICAL STUDY

BY

FRANK SWINNERTON

KENNIKAT PRESS, INC./PORT WASHINGTON, N. Y.

R.L. STEVENSON: A Critical Study

Originally published in 1915
Reissued in 1966 by Kennikat Press

Library of Congress Catalog Card No: 66-21385

TO

DOUGLAS GRAY

IN MALICE

CONTENTS

I

BIOGRAPHICAL

I

As the purpose of this book is entirely critical, and as there already exist several works dealing extensively with the life of Stevenson, the present biographical section is intentionally summary. Its object is merely to sketch in outline the principal events of Stevenson's life, in order that what follows may require no passages of biographical elucidation. Stevenson was a writer of many sorts of stories, essays, poems; and in all this diversity he was at no time preoccupied with one particular form of art. In considering each form separately, as I purpose doing, it has been necessary to group into single divisions work written at greatly different times and in greatly differing conditions. In Mr. Graham Balfour's "Life," and very remarkably in Sir Sidney Colvin's able commentaries upon Stevenson's letters, may be found information at first hand which I could only give by acts of piracy. To those works, therefore, I refer the reader who wishes to follow in chronological detail the growth of Stevenson's talent. They are, indeed, essential to all who are primarily interested in Stevenson the man. Here, the attempt will be made only to summarise the events of his days, and to estimate the ultimate value of his work in various departments of letters. This book is not a biography; it is not an "appreciation"; it is simply a critical study.

II

Stevenson was born on November 13, 1850; and he died, almost exactly forty-four years later, on December 3, 1894. His first literary work, undertaken at the age of six, was an essay upon the history of Moses. This he dictated to his mother, and was rewarded for it by the gift of a Bible picture book. It is from the date of that triumph that Stevenson's desire to be a writer must be calculated. A history of Joseph followed, and later on, apparently at the age of nine, he again dictated an account of certain travels in Perth. His first published work was a pamphlet on The Pentland Rising, written (but full of quotations) at the age of sixteen. His first "regular or paid contribution to periodical literature" was the essay called *Roads* (now included in *Essays of Travel*), which was written when the author was between twenty-two and twenty-three. The first actual book to be published was *An Inland Voyage* (1878), written when Stevenson was twenty-seven; but all the essays which ultimately formed the volumes entitled *Virginibus Puerisque* (1881) and *Familiar Studies of Men and Books* (1882) are the product of 1874 and onwards. These, indicated very roughly, are the beginnings of his literary career. Of course there were many other contributary facts which led to his turning author; and there is probably no writer whose childhood is so fully "documented" as Stevenson's. He claimed to be one of those who do not forget their own lives, and, in accordance with his practice, he has supplied us with numerous essays in which we may trace his growth and his experiences. That he was an only child and a delicate one we all know; so, too, we know that his grandfather was that Robert Stevenson who built the Bell Rock lighthouse. In the few chapters contributed by Robert Louis to *A Family of Engineers* we shall find an account, some of it fanciful, but some of it also perfectly accurate, of the Stevenson family and of Robert Stevenson, the grandfather, in particular. In *Memories and Portraits* is included a sketch of

Thomas Stevenson, the father of Robert Louis; and in Mr. Balfour's "Life" there is ample information for those who wish to study the influences of heredity.

For our own purpose it may be interesting to note three points in this connection. As a boy, and even as a youth, Stevenson was expected by his father to be an engineer and to carry on the family tradition. His early training therefore brought him much to the sea, with rather special facilities for appreciating the more active relations of man to the sea. The second point is that the Stevensons had always been, true to their Scots instincts, very strict religious disciplinarians (Robert Stevenson the elder is very illuminating on this); but that they were also very shrewd and determined men of action. Finally, another grandfather of Robert Louis, this time on the Balfour side, was in fact a clergyman. Stevenson significantly admits that he may have inherited from this grandfather the love of sermonising, which is as noticeable in *An Inland Voyage* and in *Virginibus Puerisque* as it is in his latest non-fictional work. We cannot forget that his contribution to festivities marking the anniversary of his marriage was upon one occasion a sermon on St. Jacob's Oil, delivered from a pulpit carried as part-cargo by the "Janet Nichol." From his mother, too, he is said to have inherited that constitutional delicacy which made him subject throughout his life to periods of serious illness, and which eventually led to his early death.

There was one other influence upon his childhood which must not be neglected as long as the pendulum of thought association swings steadily from heredity to environment. That influence was the influence exercised by his nurse, Alison Cunningham. It is admitted to have been enormous, and I am not sure that it is desirable to repeat in this place what is so much common knowledge. But it is perhaps worth while to emphasise the fact that, while Alison Cunningham was not only a devoted nurse, night and day, to the delicate child, she actually was in many ways responsible for the peculiar bent of Stevenson's mind. She it was who read to him, who declaimed to him, the sounds of fine words which he loved so well in after life. The meaning of the words he sometimes did not grasp; the sounds—so admirable, it would seem, was her delivery—were his deep delight. Not only that: she introduced him thus early to the Covenanting writers upon whom he claimed to have based his sense of style; and, however lightly we may regard his various affirmations as to the source of his " style," and as to the principles upon which we might expect to find it based, the sense of style, which is quite another thing, was almost certainly awakened in him by these means. Sense of style, I think, is a much greater point in Stevenson's equipment than the actual " style." The style varies ; the sense of style is constant, as it must be in any writer who is not a Freeman. Alison Cunningham, being herself possessed of this sense, or of the savour of words, impressed it upon " her boy " ; and the result we may see. All Stevenson's subsequent " learning " was so much exercise : no man learns how to write solely by observation and imitation.

From being a lonely and delicate child spinning fancies and hearing stirring words and stories and sermons in the nursery, Stevenson became a lonely and delicate child in many places. One of them was the Manse at Colinton, the home of his clerical grandfather. Another was the house in Heriot Row, Edinburgh, where he played with his brilliant cousin R. A. M. Stevenson. R.A.M. was not his only cousin—there were many others ; but the personality of R.A.M. is such that one could wish to know the whole of it, so attractive are the references in Stevenson's essays and letters, and in Mr. Balfour's biography.

I imagine, although I cannot be sure, that it was with R.A.M. that Stevenson played at producing plays on toy-stages. We shall see later how impossible he found it, when he came to consider the drama as a literary field, to shake off the influence of Skelt's drama; but anybody who has played with toy-stages will respond to the enthusiasm discovered in *A Penny Plain and Twopence Coloured*, and will sympathise with the delight which Stevenson must later have felt on being able to revive in Mr. Lloyd Osbourne's company the old Skeltian joys.

School followed in due course, the attendances broken by sickness and possibly by the incurable idleness which one supposes to have been due to lassitude rather than to mischief. Mr. Balfour details the components of Stevenson's education, from Latin and French and German, to bathing and dancing. Football is also mentioned, while riding seems to have developed into a sort of reckless horsemanship. When he was eleven or twelve Stevenson came first to London, and went with his father to Homburg. Later he went twice with Mrs. Stevenson to Mentone, travelling, besides, on the first occasion, through Italy, and returning by way of Germany and the Rhine. It is, however, remarkable that he does not seem to have retained much memory of so interesting an experience; a fact which would suggest that, although he was able at this time to store for future use ample impressions of his own feelings and his own habits, he had not yet awakened to any very lively or precise observation of the external world. That observation began with the determination to write, and Stevenson then lost no opportunity of setting down exactly his impressions of things seen.

In 1867—that is, after the publication, and after the withdrawal, of *The Pentland Rising*—Stevenson began his training as a civil engineer, working for a Science degree at Edinburgh University. One may learn something of his experience there from *Memories and Portraits* and even from *The Memoir of Fleeming Jenkin*. It was now that he met Charles Baxter (the letters to whom are the jolliest and apparently most candid of any he wrote), James Walter Ferrier, Sir Walter Simpson (the real hero of *An Inland Voyage*), and Fleeming Jenkin, whose wife mistook Stevenson for a poet. Here, too, he joined the "Speculative Society," of which presently he became an unimportant president. Moreover, the friendships formed at the University led to the foundation of a mysterious society of six members, called the L.J.R. (signifying Liberty, Justice, Reverence), which has been the occasion of much comment on account of the secrecy with which the meaning of the initials has been guarded.

It was while he was at the University that his desire to write became acute. By his own account, he went everywhere with two little books, one to read, and one to write in. He read a great deal, talked a great deal, made friends, and charmed everybody very much. In 1868, 1869, and 1870 he spent some time on the West Coast of Scotland, watching the work which was being carried on by his father's firm at Anstruther, Wick, and finally at Earraid (an island introduced into *Catriona* and *The Merry Men*). In 1871 he received from the Scottish Society of Arts a silver medal for a paper (*A New Form of Intermittent Light for Lighthouses*); and two years later another paper, *On the Thermal Influence of Forests*, was communicated to the Royal Society of Edinburgh. But it was in 1871 that Stevenson gave up, and induced his father most unwillingly to give up, the plans hitherto regarded as definite for his future career. He could not become a civil engineer; but determined that he must make his way by letters. A compromise was effected, by the terms of which he read for the Bar; and he passed his preliminary examination in 1872.

III

In 1873 Stevenson, then in great distress because of religious differences with his father, made the acquaintance of Mrs. Sitwell (now Lady Colvin) and, through her, of Sidney Colvin himself. The importance of these two friendships could hardly be over-estimated. Mrs. Sitwell gave readily and generously the sympathy of which Stevenson was so much in need; and Mr. Colvin (as he then was) proved to be, not only a friend, but a guide and a most influential champion. It was through Mr. Colvin that Stevenson made his real start as a professional writer, for Mr. Colvin was a writer and the friend of writers, a critic and the friend of—editors. Stevenson's plans for removal to London were made, and to London he came; but he was then so prostrated with nervous exhaustion, with danger of serious complications, that he was sent to the Riviera for the winter. Mr. Colvin joined him at Mentone, and introduced him to Andrew Lang. Thereafter, Stevenson went to Paris; and it was not until the end of April, 1874, that he returned to Edinburgh, apparently so far recovered that he could enjoy, three months later, a long yachting excursion on the West

Coast. Further study followed, and at length Stevenson was in 1875 called to the Scottish Bar, having been elected previously, through Mr. Colvin's kindly agency, a member of the Savile Club. Membership of the Savile led to the beginning of his association with Leslie Stephen, and to his introduction to the then editors of "The Academy" and "The Saturday Review." In this period of his life occurred the journey described in *An Inland Voyage*, and his highly important "discovery" of W. E. Henley in an Edinburgh hospital.

Finally, it is important to remember that in these full years, 1874–1879, Stevenson spent a considerable amount of time in France, where he stayed as a rule either in Paris or in the neighbourhood of Fontainebleau, most frequently at Barbizon. Details of his life in France are to be found in *The Wrecker*, in the essay called *Forest Notes* in *Essays of Travel*, and in that on *Fontainebleau* in *Across the Plains*. He was writing fairly steadily, and he was getting his work published without embarrassing difficulty, from *Ordered South* in 1874 to *Travels with a Donkey* in 1879. And it was in Grez in 1876 that he made the acquaintance of Mrs. Osbourne, an American lady separated from her husband. The meeting was in fact the turning-point in his career:

even *Travels with a Donkey*, as he admitted in a letter to his cousin, R. A. M. Stevenson, contains "lots of mere protestations to F." When Mrs. Osbourne returned to America in 1878 she sought and obtained a divorce from her husband. Stevenson heard of her intention, and heard also that she was ill. He was filled with the idea of marrying Mrs. Osbourne, and was determined to put his character to the test of so long and arduous a journey for the purpose, with the inevitable strain which his purpose involved. With perhaps a final exhibition of quite youthful affectation, and a serious misconception of his parents' attitude to himself and to the desirability of such a marriage, Stevenson took parental opposition for granted. Nevertheless, it is a proof of considerable, if unnecessary, courage, that he followed Mrs. Osbourne to California by a sort of emigrant ship and an American emigrant train. His experiences on the journey are veraciously recorded in *The Amateur Emigrant* and *Across the Plains*.

The rough, miserable journey, and the exhaustion consequent upon the undertaking of so long and difficult an expedition, brought Stevenson's vitality very low; so that, after much strain, much miscellaneous literary work, and many self-imposed privations, he fell seriously ill at San Francisco towards the end of 1879. Only careful nursing, and a genial cable from his father, promising an annual sum of £250, restored health and spirits; and on May 19, 1880, he was married to Mrs. Osbourne. Their life at Silverado has already been described in *The Silverado Squatters*; it was followed by a return to Europe, a succession of journeys from Scotland to Davos, Barbizon, Paris, and St. Germain; and a further series back again to Pitlochry and Braemar. At the last-named place *Treasure Island* was begun, and nineteen chapters of the book were written: here, too, we gather, the first poems for *A Child's Garden of Verses* laid the foundations of that book. Again, owing to bad weather in Scotland, it was found necessary to resort to Davos, where the Stevensons lived in a chalet, and where the works of the Davos Press saw the light. After a winter so spent, Stevenson was pronounced well enough to resume normal life, and he returned accordingly to England and Scotland. But before long it was necessary to go to the South of France, and after various misfortunes he settled at length at Hyères. Here he wrote *The Silverado Squatters* and resumed work on *Prince Otto*, a work long before planned as both novel and play.

Further illness succeeded, until it was found

possible to settle at Bournemouth, in the house called Skerryvore; and in Bournemouth Stevenson spent a comparatively long time (from 1884 to 1887). Here he made new friendships and revived old ones. Now were published *A Child's Garden*, *Prince Otto*, *The Dynamiter*, *Dr. Jekyll and Mr. Hyde*, and *Kidnapped*; and now, in 1887, occurred the death of Stevenson's father, of whom a sketch is given in *Memories and Portraits*.

The relations of father and son were obviously peculiar. Thomas Stevenson was strict in the matter of faith—more strict than those of this day can perhaps understand—and it is evident that this strictness provoked conflict between Robert Louis and his father. By the letters to Mrs. Sitwell we gather that the differences greatly troubled Robert Louis; but it seems very clear on the other hand that wherever the elder Stevenson's character is actively illustrated in Mr. Balfour's "Life," or in Stevenson's letters, the instance is one of kindness and consideration. Mr. Charles Baxter recalls the dreadful expression of his friend when the first draft of propositions for the L.J.R. fell into Thomas Stevenson's hands; and no doubt there is much that is personal in such stories as *Weir*, *The Wrecker*, and *John Nicholson*, in which the relations of fathers and sons are studied. That Thomas loved and admired his son seems certain; but it must be supposed that his own austerity was not always tolerable to a nature less austere and sensitive to the charge of levity.

Almost immediately after the death of his father, Stevenson left England finally. He went first to New York, and then to Saranac (in the Adirondacks), where the climate was said to be beneficial to those suffering from lung trouble. Here he began *The Master of Ballantrae* while Mr. Lloyd Osbourne was busy on *The Wrong Box*; and, when summer was returning, the whole party removed, first to New Jersey, and then to the schooner "Casco," in which they travelled to the Marquesas. In the next three years they wandered much among the groups of islands in the South Seas. *The Master of Ballantrae* was finished in a house, or rather, in a pavilion, at Waikiki, a short distance from Honolulu. It was after finishing that book that Stevenson made further journeys, until at last, by means of a trading schooner called "The Equator," the Stevensons all went to Samoa, where they settled in Apia. Here Robert Louis bought land, and built a home; and here, during the last years of his life, he lived in greater continuous health—broken though it was with occasional periods of illness more or less serious—than he had enjoyed for a number of years.

IV

At Apia he was active, both physically and in the way of authorship: his exile, trying though it must at times have been, involved health and happiness; and his loyal friends and his increasingly numerous admirers kept him, as far as they were able to do, from the dire neglect into which the thousands of miles' distance from home might suggest that he would inevitably fall. I say his loyal friends, rather than many, because Mrs. Stevenson particularly declares that Stevenson had few intimate friends. Well-wishers and admirers he had; but there is noticeable in the majority of those letters so ably collected and edited by Sir Sidney Colvin a lack of the genuine give and take of true intimacy. Information concerning himself and his doings, which suggests the use of his friends as tests or sounding-boards, forms the staple of such letters. I am told that many intimate letters are not included—for reasons which are perfectly clear and good; but the truth is that it is only in the letters to Baxter that there is any sense of great ease. Even the letters to Sir Sidney Colvin, full, clear, friendly as they are, suggest impenetrable reserves and an intense respect for the man to whom they were written. They suggest that Stevenson very much wanted Sir Sidney to go on admiring, liking, and believing in him; but they are not letters showing any deep understanding or taking-for-granted of understanding. Candour, of course, there is; a jocularity natural to Stevenson; a reliance upon the integrity and goodwill of his correspondent; a complete gratitude. All we miss is the little tick of feeling which would give ease to the whole series of letters. They might all have been written for other eyes. When one says that, one dismisses the complete spontaneity of the letters in what may seem to be an arbitrary fashion. But one is not, after all, surprised that Stevenson should have made the request that a selection of his letters should be published.

Of friends, then, there must be few, because Mrs. Stevenson is obviously in a better position than anybody else to judge upon this point. She says that, contrary to the general impression, Stevenson had few really intimate friends, because his nature was deeply reserved. From that we may infer that, like other vain men, who, however, are purged by their vanity rather than destroyed by it, he told much about himself without finally, as the phrase is, "giving himself away." His high spirits, his "bursts of confidence," his gay jocularity—all these things, part of the man's irrepressible vanity, were health to him: they enabled him to keep light in a system which might have developed, through physical delicacy, in the direction of morbidity. That he was naturally cold, in the sense that he kept his face always towards his friends, I am prepared to believe: if he had not done that he perhaps would have lost their respect, since personal charm is a fragile base for friendship. By his own family at Vailima he was accused of being "secretive," as Mrs. Strong records in "Memories of Vailima." And Stevenson, it must be remembered, was a Scotsman, with a great fund of melancholy. Quite clearly, Henley, his friend for years and his collaborator, never understood him. Henley deplored the later Stevenson, and loved the Louis (or rather, the Lewis) he had known in early days. He loved, that is, the charming person who had discovered him, and with whom he had talked and plotted and bragged. He did not love the man who seems to have turned from him. The cause of their estrangement I do not know. I imagine that they thought differently of the merits of the plays, that Henley pressed

Stevenson at a time when Stevenson felt himself to be drawing away from Henley and passing into a rather delightful isolation, and that when Henley clung to their old comradeship with characteristic vehemence, Stevenson felt suddenly bored with so loud an ally. That may be sheer nonsense : I only infer it. Whatever the cause, Stevenson seems to me always a little patronising to Henley, and Henley's attack in the "Pall Mall Magazine" (December, 1901) suggests as well as envy the blunt bewilderment of a man forsaken. Henley, of course, knew that he lacked the inventive power of Stevenson ; and he knew that his power to feel was more intense than Stevenson's. That in itself makes a sufficient explanation of the quarrel : literary friends must not be rivals, or their critical faculty will overrun into spleen at any injudicious comparisons.

Besides Henley, there is R. A. M. Stevenson, a fascinating figure ; but imperfectly shown in the "Letters." There is Sir Sidney Colvin, best and truest of friends. There is Charles Baxter, the recipient of the letters which seem to me the jolliest Stevenson wrote—a man of much joviality, I am told, and a very loyal worker on his friend's behalf. For the rest, they are friends in a general sense :

not intimates, but men whose good opinion Stevenson was proud to have earned: friends in the wide (but not the most subtle) scheme of friendship which makes for social ease and confidence and interest. Baxter and R. A. M. Stevenson were survivors of early intimacies. Mrs. Sitwell and Sir Sidney Colvin belonged to a later time, a time of stress, but a time also of growth. The others, whom we thus objectionably lump together in a single questionable word, were the warm, kind acquaintances of manhood. It is useless to demand intimacy in these cases, and I should not have laboured the point if it had not been suggested that Stevenson was one of those who had a genius for friendship. He was always, I imagine, cordial, friendly, charming to these friends; but his letters (unless we suppose Sir Sidney Colvin to have edited more freely than we should ordinarily suspect) do not seem to have much to say about his correspondents, and it is not perhaps very unreasonable to think that his own work and his own character were the basis of the exchange of letters. Stevenson no doubt liked these friends; but I am disposed to question whether he was very much interested in them. I think Stevenson generally inspired more affection than he was accustomed to give in return.

V

We must remember, in thus speaking of Stevenson's friendships, that he was a Scotsman, that he had been really a lonely child and boy, accustomed to a degree of solitude, that he was an egoist (as, presumably, all writers are egoists), and that his personal charm is unquestioned. Men who met him for the first time were fascinated by his vivacity, his fresh play of expression, his manner; and Stevenson, of course, as was only natural, responded instantly to their admiration. He was carried away in talk, and in talk walked with his new friends until they, forced as they were by other engagements to leave him, gained from such a vivid ripple of comment an impression of something alive and mercurial, something like the wonderful run of quicksilver, in a companion so inexhaustibly vivacious. It was the nervous brilliance of Stevenson which attracted men often of greater real ability; he possessed a quality which they felt to be foreign, almost dazzling. So Stevenson, leaving them, strung to a height of exhilaration by his own excited verbosity, would go upon his way, also attracted by his happy feelings and his happy phrases. In such a case the man of charm has two alternatives: he can suppress his ebullience for the purpose of learning or giving; or he can recognise the excitement and, supposing it to be lyricism, can, if I may use that word (as I have above used the word "verbosity") without any evil meaning being attached to it, *exploit* his charm. Stevenson, I believe, exploited his charm. It is often so exploited; the temptation to exploit it is sometimes irresistible. The kind thing, the attractive thing, the charming thing—this is the thing to say and do, rather than the honest thing. Instinctively a girl learns the better side of her face, the particular irresistible turn of her head, the perfect cadence of voice. So does the man who has this personal charm. So, too, does he realise instinctively the value of the external details of friendship. In only one point does the knowledge of such externals fail. The kind thing makes friends (in the sense of cordial strangers); but it does not make anything more subtle than cordial strangeness; and it does not seem to me that anybody really ever knew Stevenson very well. He told them much about himself, gaily; and they knew he was charming. I do not suggest any duplicity on his part. He was perfectly real in his vivacity, but it was nervous vivacity, an excitement that led, when it relaxed, or was relaxed, to exhaustion, possibly even to tears, just as we know that Stevenson could be carried by his own fooling to the verge of hysteria. So it was that Stevenson became a figure to himself, as well as to his friends; by his desire to continue the pleasant impression already created, he did tend to see himself objectively (just as he is said to have made the gestures he was describing in his work, and even to have gone running to a mirror to see the expression the imagined person in his book was wearing). In his early books that is plain; in *Lay Morals* we may feel that he is all the time in the pulpit, leaning over, and talking very earnestly, very gently, very persuasively, and with extraordinary self-consciousness, to a congregation that is quite clearly charmed by his personality. Above all, very persuasively; and above even his persuasiveness, the deprecating sense of charm, the use of personal anecdote to give the sermon an authentic air of confession.

The nervous, vivid buoyancy of his characteristic manner was a part of his lack of health. He was, it is known, rarely in actual pain; and it is very often the case that delicate persons have this nervous exuberance of temperament, which has almost the show of vitality. It has the show; but when the person is no longer before us, our memory is a vague, fond dream of something intangible—what we call, elusive. We talk of elusive charm when we cannot remember a single thing that has aroused in us the impression of having been charmed. Exactly in that way was Stevenson remembered by those he met—as a vivid butterfly is remembered; something indescribably strange and curious, not to be caught and held, for its brilliant and wayward fluttering. The charm was the thing that attracted men kinder, more staid, more truly genial, wiser than himself; it excused the meagre philosophisings and it excused some of those rather selfish and thoughtless actions which Mr. Balfour says nobody dreamed of resenting. The same charm we shall find in most of Stevenson's work, until it grows stale in *St. Ives*. We shall speak of its literary aspects later. At this moment we are dealing exclusively with his manner. I want to show that Stevenson's ill-health was not the ill-health which makes a man peevish through constant pain. It was, in fact, extreme delicacy, rather than ill-health; and the reaction from delicacy of physical health (or, in reality, the consequence of this delicacy) was this peculiar nervous brilliancy of manner which I have described. It is often mistaken by writers on Stevenson for courage; but this is an unimaginative conception resulting from the notion that he was constantly in pain, and that he deliberately *willed* to be cheerful and gay. Nobody who deliberately wills to be cheerful ever succeeds in being more than drolly unconvincing. Stevenson had courage which was otherwise illustrated: this cheerfulness, this "funning" was the natural consequence of nervous excitability, which, as I have said, often appears as though it was vitality, as though it must be of more substance than we know it really is. It is like the colour in an invalid's cheek, like the invalid's energy, like the invalid's bright eyes: it is due to the stimulus of excitement. Stevenson, alone, had his flat moments of dull mood and tired vanity; Stevenson, in company, thrilled with the life which his friends regarded as his inimitable and unquestionable personal charm.

You are thus to imagine a nervously-moving man, tall, very dark, very thin; his hair generally worn long; his eyes, large, dark, and bright, unusually wide apart; his face long, markedly boned. His dress, with velvet jacket, is bizarre; his whole manner is restless; his hands, skeleton-thin, constantly flickering with every change of pose. His grace of movement, his extraordinary play of expression, are everywhere commented upon by those who essay verbal portraiture; and all agree that the photographs in existence reproduce only the dead features which expression changed each instant. Stevenson, it seems, varied his position suddenly and frequently—moving from hearth-rug to chair, from chair, again, to table, walking quickly and brushing his moustache as we may see in Sargent's brilliant impression. Nervousness was in every movement, every gesture; and the figure of Stevenson seems to be recalled, by many of those who attempt the description, as invariably in motion, the face alive with interest and expression, while the man all the time talked, like "young Mr. Harry Fielding, who pours out everything he has in his heart, and is, in effect, as brilliant, as engaging, and as arresting a talker as Colonel Esmond has known."

I give the portrait for what it may be worth. No doubt it does not represent the Stevenson of Samoa; perhaps it does not represent the real Stevenson at all. It is Stevenson as one may imagine him, and as another may find it impossible to imagine him. There is room, surely, for a variety of portraits, as for the inevitable variety of critical estimates; and if the estimates hitherto have all followed a particular line of pleasant comment, at least the portraits one sees and reads are all portraits of diverse Stevensons made dull or trivial or engrossing according to the opportunities and skill of the delineator. I offer my portrait, in this and in succeeding chapters, in good faith : more, it would be impossible for me to claim.

II

JUVENILIA

I

BEFORE we come to the main divisions of Stevenson's work it may be as well to consider briefly those few early works which, to the majority of readers, were first made known by their inclusion in the Edinburgh Edition. It is unfortunately impossible to recover the original essay upon Moses, or the earliest romances; so that we are presented first with *The Pentland Rising*, published as a pamphlet when Stevenson was sixteen. This is conscientious and fully-documented work, written too close to authorities to have much flexibility or personal interest; but it is not strikingly immature. Daniel Defoe, Burnet, Fuller's "History of the Holy Warre," and a surprising number of other writers upon the period are successively quoted with good effect; and it is amusing to note the references to "A Cloud of Witnesses," which appears to have been a favourite with Alison Cunningham. This pamphlet is decidedly the outcome of Alison

Cunningham's teaching, full as it is of the authentic manner of the Covenanters, which Stevenson was presently to imitate to the admiration of all the world.

Many readers of Stevenson must have regarded with eyes of marvel the two serious papers, the gravity of which is perfect, dealing with the Thermal Influence of Forests, and with a new form of Intermittent Light. I have no ability to determine the scientific value of these papers; and as literary works they have less interest than most of the other instances of Juvenilia. They are illustrated with diagrams, and they possess coherence and lucidity. In any work these two qualities are important, and we shall find that clearness is a quality which Stevenson never lost. He always succeeded in being clear, in escaping the obscure sayings of the philosopher or the enthusiast. That is to say, he was a writer. He was a writer in those two scientific papers, no less than in *Virginibus Puerisque* or *Prince Otto*. When obscurity is so easy, clearness is a distinguished virtue; and if Stevenson sometimes errs to the extent of robbing his work of thickets and dim frightening darknesses, that is also because he was a writer, and because he preferred to be a writer.

There follow a number of shorter pieces,

some of them the fruit of his University days of practising ; some later, so that they include the papers on *Roads* and *Forest Notes* which are mentioned in the next chapter. These sometimes show obvious immaturity, but they also show more than anything else could do the real doggedness with which Stevenson pursued his aim of learning to write. They show him, at least, forming his sentences with careful attention to rhythm and to sound—not yet elaborate, not yet so " kneaded " as his manner was in a little while to be. It is here sometimes thin, as is the subject matter. In one sketch, *The Wreath of Immortelles*, we may catch a glimpse of the method of opening an essay which Stevenson developed later; but, on the other hand, in the *Forest Notes* (possibly more mature work) there is really excellent treatment of good and interesting matter. Three " criticisms " have point. One, of Lord Lytton's "Fables in Slang," is fairly conventional ; the second, on Salvini's Macbeth, was the one condemned by Fleeming Jenkin because it showed Stevenson thinking more about himself than about Salvini; the third is a very delightful little paper on Bagster's illustrated edition of "The Pilgrim's Progress."

All these short pieces are of interest because they show the growth of Stevenson as a writer.

They are the more interesting because at the same time they illustrate the way in which Stevenson gradually made his work take on the impress of his personality. All young work lacks character, as young hand-writing does, and as young style does; and all young essay-work in particular appears sometimes rather tepid and even silly when the author tries to interest us in his "ego." Stevenson from the first saw himself as the central object in his essay: it is amusing to watch how soon he begins to make himself count as an effective central object. At first the personality is thin: it has not carried. Later it develops with the development of style: the use of words becomes firmer, and with that firmness comes greater confidence, greater ease, in the projection of the author's self. It is perhaps not until we reach the familiar essays that we find Stevenson fully master of himself, for literary purposes; but the growth provides matter for rather ingenious study.

II

In that volume of the collected editions which contains these early essays it is customary to include the works issued by the Davos Press; and Mr. Lloyd Osbourne (at the age of twelve the proprietor of the Davos

Press) has also discovered a wholly amusing account of an important military campaign conducted in an attic at Davos by himself and Stevenson as opposed commanders of tin soldiers. The game, which had of course inexhaustible interest, has also, as described by Mr. Osbourne, its intricacies for the lay mind; but Stevenson's account of this particular campaign, written by means of official reports, rumours, newspapers yellow and otherwise, offers no difficulty. It is an excellent piece of pretence. The Davos Press, which provided the world with unique works by Stevenson and by Mr. Osbourne, illustrated with original woodcuts, belongs, as does the war-game, to the time spent in the châlet at Davos shortly after Stevenson's marriage. It shows how easily he could enjoy elaborate games (as most men do enjoy them, if they are not deterred by self-importance or preoccupation with matters more strictly commercial); and the relationship with Mr. Osbourne seems to have been as frank and lively as anybody could desire.

I have mentioned these matters out of their due place because they seem to me to have a value as contributing to certain suggestions which I shall make later. By his marriage, Stevenson gained not only a very devoted wife but a very intimate boy-friend, the kind of friend he very likely had long wanted. There was almost twenty years' difference between them; but that, I think, made the friendship more suited to Stevenson's nature. By means of this difference he could indulge in that very conscious make-belief for which his nature craved—a detached make-belief, which enabled him to enjoy the play both in fact and as a spectator, to make up for Mr. Osbourne's admitted superiority in marksmanship by the subtilty of his own military devices; finally, to enjoy the quite personal pleasure of placing upon record, with plans and military terms, in the best journalistic style, accounts of his military achievements. The art of gloating innocently over his own power to gloat; the power to delight consciously in his own delight at being able to play—these, I believe, are naturally Scots pleasures, and profoundly Stevensonian pleasures. I hope that no reader will deny Stevenson the right to such enjoyments, for Stevenson's not very complex nature is really bound up in them. If we take from him the satisfaction of seeing himself in every conceivable posture, we take from him a vanity which permeates his whole life-work, and which, properly regarded, is harmless to offend our taste.

III

TRAVEL BOOKS

I

"ONE of the pleasantest things in the world," says Hazlitt, "is going on a journey; but I like to go alone." In his earliest days of manhood, Stevenson also formed the habit of going alone; and in his own essay upon *Walking Tours* he very circumstantially endorses Hazlitt's view, for reasons into which we need not enter here. We may find an indication of his habit even so early as the fragment, included in *Essays of Travel*, which describes a journey from Cockermouth to Keswick. Other papers, of various dates, show that, either from choice or from necessity, he often did tramp solitary; but it is worth noting that only in the walk through the Cevennes and in his journey to America did Stevenson ever travel alone for any length of time. His other, and on the whole more important, travel-books are the descriptions of journeys taken in company.

Furthermore, in the early essay which we have just noted he rather ostentatiously proclaims his practice in writing accounts of his tours. He says, "I cannot describe a thing that is before me at the moment, or that has been before me only a little while before; I must allow my recollections to get thoroughly strained free from all chaff till nothing be except the pure gold." Apart from the surprising alchemy of the declaration, this disability is wholly to his credit; but Stevenson found, of course, that when he planned to record a journey of some duration, in a form more or less chronological, he must preserve a sense of fabric in his book by keeping a daily diary of experiences. That is why, in his earliest book of travel, *An Inland Voyage*, he mentions "writing-up" his diary at the end of each day; and it explains also the frequent references in later books to such an evening occupation. As Stevenson admitted in *Cockermouth and Keswick*, the process of incubation might in the long run be unreasonably prolonged; and perhaps it is true that experience taught him very early that in the professional writer thrift is a virtue. It was, if so, a lesson that he never forgot.

Although the fragment on Keswick to which I have referred is clearly a juvenile piece of work, it is highly entertaining as a small piece of autobiography. On its own account the essay is rather pragmatical and anecdotal, after the manner of an afternoon sermon, and it gives as yet small evidence that the writer has any highly developed sense of accurate and significant observation. But to the reader who cares to go below its superficial interest, there is other material. Not without value are the boyish allusions to his pipe, to his whisky-and-soda, and to his importance in the smoking-room of the hotel. These are all typical, and interesting. What, however, is clear on the question of mere literary talent, is Stevenson's ability to spin something out of himself. He must be talking; and, if he has nothing of much moment to say, there must follow some apt reflection, or a "tale of an old Scots minister."

Would that the ability, a very dangerous ability, had been shed as soon as were some of Stevenson's juvenile theories about the art of writing! This particular ability remains very noticeably in his first full-size travel-book, *An Inland Voyage*, along with another trait—his abnormal consciousness of his own appearance in the eyes of other people. Stevenson was always interested in that aspect of his personality: he could not forget for a moment that his costume, his face, his manner, all carried some impression to the beholder. It was a part of his nature that he should see children upon the river bank, not merely as children, but as an audience, a congregation of speculating souls busy wondering about him, likening him among themselves to some particular figure, interested in him. Nobody, I think, had ever failed to be interested in him.

II

An Inland Voyage, on the whole, is a poor book. It records a canoeing expedition made with a friend; and it is full of Puritanical obtuseness and a strained vanity which interferes with the main narrative. Setting out from Antwerp, the two friends paddled, often in the rain, and sometimes—as in the case of Stevenson's arrest, and his dangerous accident with the fallen tree across the swollen Oise—in dire straits. They travelled on the Sambre and down the Oise by Origny and Moy, Noyon, Compiègne, and Précy; but the weather was bad, and there were trying difficulties about lodgings; and Stevenson's account reads as though he had been chilled through and through, and as though he needed nothing so much as his home. Almost invariably, in this book, his little spurts of epigram and apophthegm suggest low spirits as well as a sort of cautious experimentalism; and the book, which apparently was very handsomely received by the Press on its publication, is eked out with matter which, beneath the nervous delicacy of Stevenson's practising style, is raw and sometimes *banale*. In no other travel-book is there shown such obvious effort. What emerges from *An Inland Voyage* is the charmingly natural behaviour on several occasions of Stevenson's companion, a proof even thus early of the author's ability to be aware of these traits in his friends which, on the printed page, convey to the reader an impression of the person so lightly sketched. This, however, is an exiguous interest in a book supposed to be a picturesque work of travel and topography.

Very much superior is the Sternian *Travels with a Donkey*. Here there is much greater lightness of touch, and a really admirable sense of observation is revealed. Some of the descriptions of things seen are written with indescribable delicacy, as are the character sketches. Just so are some of the descriptions of places contained in the series of letters to Mrs. Sitwell. In *Travels with a Donkey* for the first time the reader actually makes a third with Stevenson and the endearing Modestine upon their journey, travelling with them and sharing the sensations of the human pedestrian. If we resent certain intolerable affectations—such as the pretentious and penurious fancy of placing money by the roadside in payment for lodgings in the open air—that resentment may be partly due to the fact that we are not told the amount of the payment, as well, of course, as to the fact that we suspect the author's motive in detailing his charities. Stevenson seems, in fact, to be asking for commendation of a fantastic generosity without giving us sufficient evidence to evoke any feeling of conviction. We see him here, not so much obeying a happy impulse as observing himself in the light of his own esteem ; and that is hardly a pleasant sight to the onlooker. To counterbalance such lapses—which, very likely, are regarded by lovers of Stevenson as no lapses at all, but as delightful exhalations of personality, as glimpses of his character which they are enabled to enjoy only through this very innocent vanity which we have noted,—there are a thousand graceful touches, fit to remind us that *Travels with a Donkey* is a much better book than *An Inland Voyage*, and, in fact, the best of his travel-books until we reach that delightfully modest one which is too little known—*The Silverado Squatters.* The *Donkey* is the first in which the charming side of his personality really "gets going," and it will always remain a pretty and effective sketch of a journey taken in wayward weather, with good spirits, a shrewd and observant eye, and, what is also to the point, a commendable courage.

The Amateur Emigrant and *Across the Plains*, two long records which, although published separately, are practically a single work, for all their difference from that book are a drop to the executive level of *An Inland Voyage.* Here again Stevenson was affected by the discomforts of his lonely travelling, and no doubt by his poor health. Both records are for the most part superficial and crabbed. The descriptions of travelling-companions are conscientious, but they have, as Stevenson's earliest admirers were the first to remark, no imagination or genuine moulding: the accounts are a good deal like uninspired letters home. If one thinks what Stevenson, in happy circumstances, might have made of the tale of his journey, one realises how lifeless are the descriptions given. They have no sense of actual contact; they have lost grip in losing charm, and might have been written by somebody with far less of an eye to the significance of the passing scene. Stevenson claimed to have been aware of the prosaic character of the records, and, indeed, in one letter to Sir Sidney Colvin he said, "It bored me hellishly to write; well, it's going to bore others to read; that's only fair." So perhaps it is not worth while to analyse such confessedly inferior works. Only once in *The Amateur Emigrant*—in the anecdote of two men who lodged perilously in New York—does Stevenson's boyish love of the picturesquely terrible bring a note of tense reality to the writing. In its own way the account of the two men looking from their bedroom, through the frame of a seeming picture, into another room where three men are crouching in darkness, is a little masterpiece of horror. It belongs to his romances rather than to his travel-books; but it is the passage that stands out most distinctly from the two which are under notice at the moment. No other scene in either *The Amateur Emigrant* or *Across the Plains* compares with it for interest or value.

III

Following upon his tedious journey to America, and the hardships and illness which, before his marriage, brought him nearly to his grave, Stevenson went to the mountains for health. *The Silverado Squatters* was written-up later, and, from Stevenson's letters of that time, it seems to have been condemned as uncharacteristic. But it may have been that, as I think was the case, Stevenson's voyage to America and his marriage considerably affected his outlook. For one thing he really had come into contact with hard inconvenience and loneliness, with a self-inflicted exile from his family (and a hostility to his marriage on their part which existed more in his imagination than in fact), which matured him. Those of us who never take these voyages out into the unknown, who sit tight and think comfortably of such things as emigrant trains, cannot realise with what sudden effect the stubborn impact of realities can work upon those who actually venture forth. One small instance will show something of the experience Stevenson gained. On the voyage he met emigrants who were leaving Scotland because there was nothing else for them to do, because to stay meant "to starve." Coming to these men, and hearing from them something of the lives they had left, he touched a new aspect of life which, in spite of his runnings to-and-fro in Edinburgh and elsewhere, he had never appreciated. He writes, in *The Amateur Emigrant*:

> I had heard vaguely of these reverses; of whole streets of houses standing deserted by the Tyne, the cellar-doors broken and removed for firewood; of homeless men loitering at the street-corners of Glasgow with their chests beside them; of closed factories, useless strikes, and starving girls. But I had never taken them home to me or represented these distresses livingly to my imagination.

And when, in *Across the Plains*, he tells how his emigrant train, going in one direction, crowded, was met by another, also crowded, *returning*, must that not have reacted upon his mind? My own impression, which of course is based upon nothing more than the apparent change in Stevenson's manner of writing, is that *The Silverado Squatters*, as we now have it, very much altered from the condemned first drafts, represents the emergence of a new Stevenson, who, in *The Amateur Emigrant* and *Across the Plains*, had been overweighted by the material realities he had in bad health encountered, and who, in consequence, had failed to make those accounts vivid. *The Silverado Squatters* has more substance than its predecessors. It is much more free, it is almost entirely free, from affectation. The style is less full of trope, and may be considered therefore, by some readers, as the less individual. But the matter and manner are more strictly united than hitherto. We are not interrupted by such trivial explosions of sententiousness as "We must all set our pocket-watches by the clock of Fate," and in the degree in which the matter entirely "fills-out" the manner the book is so far remarkable. It is not generally regarded as convenient to say that Stevenson's matter was often thin, and his style a mere ruffle and scent to draw off the more frigid kind of reader; yet when we come to work so able and so unpretentious as *The Silverado Squatters*, in which Stevenson is honestly trying to show what he saw and knew (instead of trying to show the effect of his address upon a strange community) we do seem to feel that what has gone before has been less immediately the natural work of the writer, and more the fancy sketch of the writer's own sense of his picturesque figure. In one aspect, in its lack of vivacity, *The Silverado Squatters* may compare to disadvantage with earlier work; it may seem, and indeed is ordinarily condemned as, less pungent, and less elastic; but that could only be to those who miss the fact that Stevenson's pungency and elasticity were the consequence of the unwearying revision to which most of his work was subjected. He was never a quick worker, never one of those careless writers whose ear approves while the pen is in motion. He had a fine ear, but not essentially a quick ear; he was not what is sometimes called a "natural" writer, but with devoted labour went again and again through what he had written, revising it until his fastidiousness was relieved. This way of working, while it served to allay what he called the "heat of composition"—a heat which some readers find very grateful in other, less painstaking writers—has patent virtues. It is likely to make work more polished and more finely balanced. Nevertheless, it probably has the effect of reducing the vigour and resilience of a style. However that may be, it is a method making great demands upon a writer's deep conscientiousness; and it is not the purpose of this book to extol the rapid method or the quick ear. All we may do at this moment is to suggest that Stevenson, having done well in practising year after year the craft of the writer, had now turned very deliberately and honourably in the first year of his marriage to that other side of the writer's craft, the sober description, free from the amateur's experimentalism, of the real world as he saw it. Even so, it is a world made smooth by his temperament—his love of smoothness, which one may see exemplified in his declared love of simple landscape—and by his matured dexterity in manipulating sentences. It is a world seen, not with rich vitality, but with the friendly interest of one in a fair haven, whose imagination is not fierce enough to be a torture to him. Stevenson heard, saw, and really felt his surroundings; his descriptions of sudden beauties here at Silverado, as later in Samoa, have the quiet religious character which distinguished all his truest intuitions of beauty. Not his the ecstatic oneness with the lovely things of Nature which makes Keats the purest exponent of what Keats himself called "that delicate snail's-horn perception of beauty": Stevenson's ecstasy had to be stirred by excitement; he had not the poet's open-handed out-running to the emotion of place. But his sense of the remoteness of the squatters of Silverado, his early-morning peeps into the wonders of colour and aspect in a strange corner of the earth, his shrewd understanding of sullen human nature, are made clear to the reader by plain expression. The book is self-conscious in a good sense; not, as has often hitherto been the case, in a bad one.

IV

If we notice such a change of attitude in *The Silverado Squatters*, we shall find it even more fully revealed in the volume of his letters for an American magazine which appeared under the title of *In the South Seas.* Some of the letters were withheld, as too tedious; even now, the book is frankly called dull by many staunch admircrs of Stevenson. To others, however, it must surely appear otherwise. It is, in effect, a sort of glorified log; but a log of real enterprise and adventure in a marvellous part of the world. Stevenson heroically tried to penetrate to the heart of the South Seas. He was caught up by the islands and their people, and was bent upon making them known to those who lived afar. In the political intrigues so honestly described in his letters, Stevenson may, indeed, appear to throw away the importance of his own genius; but the sacrifice is made in obedience to his deepest convictions of right. He still sees himself as the point of focus; but we do not resent that when we find ourselves so clearly in his train. Even while his friends were urging him to give up the Samoan politics which threatened to become the King Charles's head of his correspondence, he continued to live amid the difficulties from which he felt that he could not in honour withdraw. And although the Samoan period had its fluctuations of talent, it was, upon the whole, the time when his boyish love of game took on a keener zest of earnest and made him indeed a man. The period marks a further decline in the more strictly romantic nature of his work, as we may later on be able to discuss in comparing *St. Ives* with earlier and more triumphant experiments in that field; but it opens the path for the sober realism (if that word may here be used without sinister connotation) of the torso known as *Weir of Hermiston*, a fragment in which it is usual to find the greatest promise of all. This is all of a piece with the increasing purpose of Stevenson's way in life. It is a good sign when a professional author forsakes romance in favour of reality; for romance may be conjured for bread-and-butter, while reality withstands the most persuasive cajollery. Stevenson was the professional author in his collaborations, and in such work as *St. Ives*; but in *In the South Seas* as in *Weir* he is writing truth for the love of truth, than which there can be no more noble kind of authorship.

V

In San Francisco, as we have seen, Stevenson chartered a schooner-yacht, and went to the South Seas in pursuit of health. On board ship he was always happy; and he made more than one cruise, in different ships, among the Gilbert, Paumotuan, and Marquesan groups of islands. He also stayed for periods of varying length in the three groups of islands, became familiar with the manners of the natives, realised their distinctions, and made many new friends among them. His mind was entirely occupied with them; he saw everything he could, and learned everything he could, his shrewd Scots habit of inquiry filling him with a satisfied sense of labour. A big book, proving beyond doubt the entire peculiarity of the South Sea islands and their islanders, was planning in his mind; a book which would soundly establish his reputation as something other than a literary man and a teller of tales. *In the South Seas*, as I have already mentioned, was found dull by friendly critics; yet it is full of observation and of feeling. It is the wisest of the travel books, and the most genuine, for Stevenson has put picturesqueness behind him for what it is—the hall-mark of the second-rate writer; and he has risen to a height of understanding which adds to his stature. There is, in the portrait of Tembinok', a simplicity which is impressive: throughout, there is a simple exposition of a fascinating subject, a kind of life remote from our experience, a civilisation strict and dignified, minds and habits interesting in themselves and by contrast with our own. The book may not be the epitome of the South Seas for which the chapters were planned as rough notes; other writers may have known more than Stevenson knew of the actual life of the islands. It is true that he frequented kings' palaces, and that his acquaintance with common native life was very largely a matter of observation caught up in passing, or by hearsay, or by the contemplation of public gatherings. That is true. What we, as readers endeavouring patiently to trace the growth of Stevenson's knowledge, must, however, remember above all things, is that the book is really a finer and a more distinguished work than *An Inland Voyage* or *Travels with a Donkey*. It has not the grimaces of the first, or the pleasing delicacy of the second. It is a better book than *The Amateur Emigrant* and *Across the Plains*. It is fuller and richer than *The Silverado Squatters*. What, then, do we ask of a book of travel? Is it that we may see the author goading his donkey, or putting money by the wayside for his night's lodging; or is it that we may see what he has seen? With Stevenson, the trouble is, I suppose, that, having thought of him always as a dilettante, his admirers cannot reconcile themselves to his wish to be a real traveller and a real historian. Perhaps they recognise that he had not the necessary equipment? Rather, it is very likely that, being largely uncreative themselves, they had planned for Stevenson a future different from the one into which gradually he drifted. All creative writers have such friends. We may say, perhaps, that a man who was not Stevenson could have written *In the South Seas*, though I believe that is not the case. But if we put the books slowly in order we shall almost certainly find that while *Travels with a Donkey* is a pretty favourite, with airs and graces, and a rather imaginary figure charmingly posed as its chief attraction, *In the South Seas* is the work of the same writer, grown less affected, more intent upon seeing things as they are, and less intent upon being seen in their midst. There is the problem. If a travel-book is an exploitation of the traveller's self, we can be charmed with it: let us not, therefore, because we find less charm in *In the South Seas*, find the later book dull. Stevenson is duller because he is older: the bloom is going: he is not equal intellectually to the task he has set himself. But there is a greater sincerity in the later travel books, an honest looking upon the world. It is surely better to look straight with clear eyes than to dress life up in a bundle of tropes and go singing up the pasteboard mountain. Stevenson's admirers want the song upon the mountain, because they want to continue the legend that he never grew up. They want him to be the little boy with a fine night of stars in his eyes and a pack upon his back, singing cheerily that it is better to travel hopefully than to arrive. That is why Stevenson's best work is, relatively speaking, neglected in favour of work that tarnishes with the passing of youth. And it is all because of the insatiable desire of mediocrity for the picturesque. We must be surprised and startled, and have our senses titillated by savours and perfumes; we must have the strange and the new; we must have a fashion to follow and to forget. Stevenson has been a fashionable traveller, and his sober maturity is too dull; he has lost his charm. Well, we must make a new fashion. Interest in a figure must give place to interest in the work. If the work no longer interests, then our worship of Stevenson is founded upon a shadow, is founded, let us say, upon the applause of his friends, who sought in his work the fascination they found in his person.

IV

ESSAYS

I

There have been some English essayists whose writing is so packed with thought that it is almost difficult to follow the thought in its condensation. Such was Bacon, whose essays were by way of being "assays," written so tightly that each little sentence was the compression of the author's furthest belief upon that aspect of his subject, and so that to modern students the reading of Bacon's essays resembles the reading of a whole volume printed in Diamond type. There have been English essayists whose essays are clear-cut refinements of truth more superficial or more simple. Such was Addison, who wrote with a deliberate and flowing elegance, and whose essays Stevenson found himself unable to read. There have been such essayists as Hazlitt, the shrewd sincerity of whose perceptions is expressed with so much appropriateness that his essays are examples of what essays should be. There has never been in England a critic or an essayist of quite the same calibre as Hazlitt. It was of Hazlitt that Stevenson wrote, in words so true that they summarily arrest by their significance the reader who does not expect to find in *Walking Tours* so vital an appraisement: "Though we are mighty fine fellows nowadays, we cannot write like Hazlitt." And, in succession, for there would be no purpose in continuing the list for its own sake, there have been essayists who, intentionally resting their work upon style and upon the charm of personality, have in a thousand ways diversified their ordinary experience, and so have been enabled to disclose as many new aspects and delights to the reader. Such an essayist was Lamb. Hazlitt, I think, was the last of the great English essayists, because Hazlitt sought truth continuously and found his incomparable manner in the disinterested love of precision to truth. But Lamb is the favourite; and Lamb is the English writer of whom most readers think first when the word "essay" is mentioned. That is because Lamb brought to its highest pitch that personal and idiosyncratic sort of excursion among memories which has created the modern essay, and which has severed it from the older traditions of both Bacon and Addison. It is to the school of

Lamb, in that one sense, that Stevenson belonged. He did not " write for antiquity," as Lamb did; he did not write deliberately in the antique vein or in what Andrew Lang called " elderly English " ; but he wrote, with conscious and anxious literary finish, essays which had as their object the conveyance in an alluring manner of his own predilections. He quite early made his personality what Henley more exactly supposed that it only afterwards became — a marketable commodity — as all writers of strong or acquired personality are bound to do.

Since Stevenson there have been few essayists of classic rank, largely because the essay has lost ground, and because interest in " pure " literature has been confined to work of established position (by which is meant the work of defunct writers). There has been Arthur Symons, of whose following of Pater as an epicure of sensation we have heard so much that the original quality of his fine work—both in criticism and in the essay—has been obscured. There has been an imitator of Stevenson, an invalid lady using the pseudonym " Michael Fairless " ; and there have been Mr. Max Beerbohm, Mr. E. V. Lucas, Mr. Belloc, Mr. Chesterton, Mr. Street, Mr. A. C. Benson, and Mr. Filson Young. These writers have all been of the " personal " school, frankly accepting the essay as the most personal form in literature, and impressing upon their work the particular personal qualities which they enjoy. Some of them have been more robust than others, some less distinguished; but all of them are known to us (in relation to their essays) as writers of personality rather than as writers of abstract excellence. An essay upon the art of the essay, tracing its development, examining its purpose, and distinguishing between its exponents, might be a very fascinating work. Such an essay is manifestly out of place here; but it is noteworthy that, apart from the distinguished writers whose names I have given, nearly all the minor writers (that is, nearly all those whose names I have not mentioned) who have produced essays since the death of Stevenson, or who are nowadays producing genteel essays, have been deeply under his influence. It is further noteworthy that most of those who have been so powerfully influenced have been women.

II

From the grimly earnest abstracts of knowledge contributed by Bacon to the art of the essay, to the dilettante survey of a few fancies, or memories, or aspects of common truth which ordinarily composed a single essay by Stevenson, is a far cry. But Stevenson, as I have said, belonged to the kind of essayist of whom in England Charles Lamb is most representative, and of whom Montaigne was most probably his more direct model—the writer who conveyed information about his personal tastes and friends and ancient practices in a form made prepossessing by a flavoured style. To those traits, in Stevenson's case, was added a strong didactic strain, as much marked in his early essays as in the later ones; and it is this strain which differentiates Stevenson's work from that of Lamb and Montaigne. Montaigne's essays are the delicious vintage of a ripe mind both credulous and sceptical, grown old enough to examine with great candour and curiousness the details of its own vagaries: many of Stevenson's most characteristic essays are the work of his youth, as they proclaim by the substitution of the pseudo-candour of vanity for the difficult candour of Montaigne's shrewd naïveté. He was thirty or thirty-one when the collection entitled *Virginibus Puerisque* was published. A year later there followed *Familiar Studies of Men and Books*. He was only thirty-seven (Montaigne was thirty-eight when he "retired" from active life and began to produce his essays) when his third collection, *Memories and Portraits*, obviously more sedate and less open to the charge of literary affectation, completed the familiar triology. Although *Across the Plains* did not appear until 1892, many of the essays which help to form that book had earlier received periodical publication (the dated essays range from 1878 to 1888); while some of the papers posthumously collected in *The Art of Writing* belong to 1881. So it is not unfair to say that the bulk of Stevenson's essays were composed before he reached the age of thirty-five ; and thirty-five, although it is an age by which many writers have achieved fame, is not quite the age by which personality is so much matured as to yield readily to condensation. Therefore we must not look, in Stevenson's essays, for the judgments of maturity, although we may find in *Virginibus Puerisque* a rather middle-aged inexperience. We must rather seek the significance of these essays in the degree in which they reveal consciously the graces and the faultless negligé of an attractive temperament. We may look to find at its highest point the illustration of those principles of style which Stevenson endeavoured to formulate in one very careful essay upon the subject (to the chagrin, I seem to remember, at the time of its republication, of so many critics who misunderstood the aim of the essay). And we shall assuredly find exhibited the power Stevenson possessed of quoting happily from other writers. Quotation with effect is a matter of great skill; and Stevenson, although his reading was peculiar rather than wide, drew from this very fact much of the inimitable effect obtained by references so apt.

III

One note which we shall find persistently struck and re-struck in Stevenson's essays is the memory of childhood. From *Child's Play* to *The Lantern-Bearers* we are confronted by a mass of material regarding one childhood, by which is supported a series of generalisations about all children and their early years. So we proceed to youth, to the story of *A College Magazine*; and so to *Ordered South*. Then we return again to *An Old Scotch Gardener* and *The Manse*, where again that single childhood, so well-stored with memories, provides the picture. Now it is one thing for Stevenson to re-vivify his own childhood, for that is a very legitimate satisfaction which nobody would deny him; but it is another thing for Stevenson, from that single experience and with no other apparent observation or inquiry, to generalise about all children. While he tells us what he did, in what books and adventures and happenings he found his delight, we may read with amusement. When, upon the other hand, he says, "children are thus or thus," it is open to any candid reader to disagree with Stevenson. Whether it is that he has set the example, or whether it is that he merely exemplifies the practice, I cannot say; but Stevenson is one of those very numerous people who talk wisely and shrewdly about children in the bulk without seeming to know anything about them. These wiseacres alternately underrate and make too ingenious the intelligence and the calculations of childhood, so that children in their hands seem to become either sentimental barbarians or callous schemers, but are never, in the main, children at all. Stevenson has a few excellent words upon children: he admirably says, "It is the grown people who make the nursery stories; all the children do, is jealously to preserve the text": but I am sorry to say that, upon the whole, I can find little else that is of value in his general observations.

It is open to anybody to reconstruct a single real childhood from Stevenson's essays, and no doubt that is a matter of considerable interest, as anything which enables us to understand a man is of value. Curiously enough, however, Stevenson's essays upon the habits and notions of children seem to suggest a great deal too much thought about play, and too little actual play. They seem to show him, as a little boy, so precocious and lacking in heart, that he is watching himself play rather than playing. It is not the preliminary planning of play that delights children, not the academic invention of games and deceits; it is the immediate and enjoyable act of play. Our author shows us a rather elderly child who, in deceiving himself, has savoured not so much the game as the supreme cleverness of his own self-deception. That, to any person who truly remembers the state of childhood, may be accepted as a perfectly legitimate recollection; and it is so far coherent. That his own habit should be, in these essays, extended to all other children whatsoever—in fact, to "children"—is to make all children delicate little Scots boys, greatly loved, very self-conscious, and, in the long run, rather tiresome, as lonely, delicate little boys incline to become towards the end of the day. Unfortunately the readers of Stevenson's essays about little boys have mostly been little girls; and they are not themselves children, but grown-up people who are looking back at their own childhood through the falsifying medium of culture and indulgent, dishonest memory. Culture, in dwelling upon interpretations and upon purposes, and in seeing childhood always through the refraction of consequence, destroys interest in play itself; and if play is once called in question it very quickly becomes tedious rigmarole.

Stevenson's essays must thus be divided into two parts, the first descriptive, the second generalised. The first division, sometimes delightful, is also sometimes sophisticated, and sometimes is exaggerative of the originality of certain examples of play. The second is about as questionable as any writing on children has ever been, because it is based too strictly upon expanded recollections of a single abnormal model. You do not, by such means, obtain good generalisations.

IV

Something of the same objection might be urged against Stevenson's rather unpleasant descriptions of adolescence. These again are not typical. Stevenson himself was the only youth he ever knew—he never had the detachment to examine disinterestedly the qualities of any person but himself—and we might gain from his descriptions an impression of youth which actually will not bear the stereoscopic test to which we are bound to submit all generalisations. To read the essays with the ingenuous mind of youth is to feel wisdom, grown old and immaculate, passing from author to reader. It is to marvel at this debonair philosopher, who finds himself never in a quandary, and who has the strategies of childhood and of youth balanced in his extended hand. It is to proceed from childhood to youth, and from youth to the married state; and our adviser describes to us in turn, with astonishing confidence, the simplified relations, which otherwise we might have supposed so intricate, of the lover, the husband, and the wife. Nothing comes amiss to him: love, jealousy, the blind bow-boy, truth of intercourse—these and many other aspects of married life are discoursed upon with grace and the wistful sagaciousness of a decayed inexperience. But when we consider the various arguments, and when we bring the essays *Virginibus Puerisque* back to their starting-point, we shall find that they rest upon the boyish discovery that marriages occur between unlikely persons. Stevenson has not been able to resist the desire to institute an inquiry into the reasons. He cannot suppose that these persons love one another; and yet why else should they marry? Well, he is writing an essay, and not a sociological study, so that—as the result of his inquiry—we must not expect to receive a very distinct contribution to our knowledge. We may prepare only to be edified, to be, perhaps, greatly amused by a young man who may at least shock us, or stir us, if he is unable to show this fruitful source of comedy in action. We are even, possibly, alert to render our author the compliment of preliminary enjoyment, before we have come to his inquiry. What Stevenson has to tell us about marriage, however, is a commonplace; even if it is a commonplace dressed and flavoured. It is that "marriage is a field of battle—not a bed of roses"; and it is that "to marry is to domesticate the Recording Angel." "Alas!" as Stevenson says of another matter, "If that were all!"

I wonder what it is that makes such phrases (for they are no more than phrases, phrases which are not true to experience, and which therefore can have no value as propositions or as explanations) give so much pleasure to such a number of readers. How can we explain it, unless it be simply by the explanation that Stevenson has been idolised? This book, *Virginibus Puerisque*, has been a favourite for many years, sanguine, gentle, musical, in the deepest sense unoriginal. It is the most quoted; it is the one which most certainly may be regarded as the typical book of Stevenson's early period. Surely it is because a half-truth, a truth that may be gobbled up in a phrase and remembered only as a phrase, is easier to accept than a whole truth, upon which the reader must engage his attention? It must, I mean, be the trope that lures readers of *Virginibus Puerisque* into acceptance of thought so threadbare and ill-nourished. Such an essay as *Æs Triplex* seems by its air to hold all the wisdom of the ages, brought steadfastly to the contemplation of the end to which all must come. If it is read sentimentally, with the mind swooning, it may give the reader the feeling that he has looked upon the bright face of danger and seen death as no such bad thing. For a moment, as it might be by a drug, he has received some stimulation which is purely temporary. The essay has not changed his thought of death; it has not transformed his fear of death into an heroic love; it slides imperceptibly, unheeded, from his memory, and remains dishevelled for ever as "that rather fine thing of Stevenson's," for which he never knows where to look. Only its phrases remain for quotation, for use in calendars, common thoughts turned into remembrances and mottoes ready for the rubricator. When an ordinary person says, "It's nice to have something to look forward to," Stevenson is ready with, "It is better to travel hopefully than to arrive, and the true success is to labour." There is all the difference between this and that advice of Browning's that "a man's reach should exceed his grasp." Stevenson has not sought to invigorate the toiler, he has not caught up with optimism the spirit of mankind: what he has done is to make a phrase for the boudoir. There is no philosophic optimism in Stevenson's essays: there is sometimes high spirits, and sometimes there is a cheerful saying; but at heart the "teaching" of these things is as prosaic as is the instruction of any lay preacher.

When the more solemn sort of subject, such as death, comes to be dealt with, we find Stevenson, the actor, falling into the feeling of his own intonations, gravely reassuring, like a politician explaining a defeat. When he is describing acts of bravery, as in *The English Admirals*, his love of courage rises and his feelings seem to glow; but the phrases with which he adorns the tale and with which eventually he points the moral are phrases made to be read, not phrases that break from his full heart. They are not the phrases made, will he nill he, by his enthusiasm; they are such phrases as are publicly conveyed from one king or statesman or commander to another upon the occasion of some notable event. I do not mean that they are as baldly expressed, though I think they are often as baldly conceived. They are very handsomely expressed, too handsomely for the occasion, if one agrees with Bob Acres that "the sound should be an echo of the sense." Although it may be true that, as Stevenson says, "people nowhere demand the picturesque so much as in their virtues," for a self-respecting author to give them the picturesque for that reason seems to me a most immoral and, in the end, a most ill-judged proceeding. Cultivation of the picturesque, fondness for phrase, is inevitably productive of falseness; it is literary gesture, a cultivable habit, such as the habit of any vain person who flickers his hands or persistently turns the "better side" of his face or character to the beholder. The first instinctive vanity develops rapidly into a pose, and pose can never be much more than amusing. Appropriateness of phrase to meaning is lost in the sense of phrase, honesty of intention does not suffice to cover inexactitude of expression. Unconsciously, Stevenson often approved a phrase that expressed something not in exact accordance with his belief; he was misled by its splendour or its picturesqueness or its heroic virtue. So it is that the parts of Stevenson's essays which at first drew and held us breathless with a sort of wonder, cease at length to awaken this wonder, and even seem to degenerate into exhibitions of knack, as though they were the sign of something wholly artificial in the writer. They grow tedious, like the grimaces of a spoilt child; and we no longer respond to that spurious galvanism which of old we mistook for a thrill of nature.

To Stevenson's less elaborate essays the mind turns with greater pleasure. We are displeased in *Virginibus Puerisque* by the excess of manner over matter: wherever the matter is original the manner is invariably less figured. Our trouble then is that, as in the case of such essays as *The Foreigner at Home* and *Pastoral*, where the matter is of great interest, there is produced the feeling that Stevenson has not developed it to its fullest extent. His essay on the English, to take the first of the two we have named, is partial and incomplete —faults due to lack of sympathy. Its incompleteness seems to me more serious than its partiality; and by "incompleteness" I do not mean that it should have been more exhaustive, but that it does not appear quite to work out its own thesis, but presents an air of having been finished on a smaller scale than is attempted in other parts. In exactly the same way, the *Pastoral* engages our interest completely, and then, for the reason, it would seem, that the author's memory runs short, the portrait is left suddenly. It is not left in such a state that the reader's imagination fills in every detail: the effect is again one of truncation.

The best of these essays are probably those two, which are written in the vein of Hazlitt, on *Talk and Talkers*. Here the matter is ample; and the manner is studiously moderate. I note, by the way, that Sir Sidney Colvin mentions the composition of this essay at about the time of Stevenson's proposal for writing a life of Hazlitt; so that it would not be very reckless to say that the manner of *Talk and Talkers* may be due to a contemporary familiarity with Hazlitt's essays. However that may be, these two essays in particular have distinguished qualities. They have point, character, and thought.

V

The two essays which conclude *Memories and Portraits*, respectively entitled *A Gossip on Romance* and *A Humble Remonstrance*, are by way of being essays in constructive criticism, showing why the novel of incident (i.e. the romance) is superior to the domestic novel. The former belongs to 1882, the latter to 1884. *A Gossip on Romance* expresses for "Robinson Crusoe" a greater liking than that held for "Clarissa Harlowe," and concludes with great praise of Scott; *A Humble Remonstrance* shows Stevenson entering, with something of the *Father Damien* manner, into a debate which was at that time taking place between Sir Walter Besant, Mr. Henry James, and Mr. W. D. Howells. Besant's arguments were contained in an essay on "The Art of Fiction," which may still be had as a negligible little book; Mr. Henry James's reply, a wholly delightful performance, is reprinted in "Partial Portraits." The point was that Besant wanted to express his amiable and workmanlike notions, that Mr. Henry James preferred to talk about the *art* of fiction, and that Stevenson, who seems never to have felt entire approval of the subject-matter of Mr. James's books, felt called upon to rally to the defence of his own practices. Unfortunately he could not do this without savaging Mr. James and Mr. Howells, and this, while it makes the essay a rather honest, unaffected piece of work, does not increase its lucidity.

But we may very well turn at this point to notice that Stevenson's one legitimate book of essays on specifically literary subjects—*Familiar Studies of Men and Books*—illustrates very well his attitude to the writers in whom he was interested to the point of personal study. The nine subjects of the essays in this book do not seem to us at this time a specially interesting selection; and indeed the essays themselves are not remarkable for originality or insight. It does show, however, some range of understanding to wish to write upon subjects so varied as Hugo, Burns, Whitman, Thoreau, Villon, Charles of Orleans, Pepys, and John Knox. It is true that Stevenson (the Hugo essay is perhaps an exception to this) never gets very far away from his "authorities" or from quotations from the works of his subject; and that his criticism is "safe" rather than personal; but these facts, while they interfere with the value of the essays as essays, give them the interest of being single and without parallel in Stevenson's output. They show that he was a good enough journeyman critic to stand beside those who write essays on literary subjects for the reviews. They conform, as far as I can tell, to the standard of such work; they are useful and plain, and some of them, but not all, are interesting. In each case the interest is chiefly a moral interest; it is the "teaching" of the various writers, the moral vagaries of the different delinquents, that engage the critic's attention.

It must be borne in mind that Stevenson was not primarily a literary critic. His flashes of insight were more remarkable than his considered judgments, because, as I have suggested elsewhere in this book, he had not the kind of mind that takes delight in pursuing a subject to its logical conclusion. He had the inventive, but not the constructive mind, and he had the nervous and delicate man's intolerance of anything requiring sustained intellectual effort. I imagine that in reading books he "read for the story," and that his perception of qualities in the telling (apart from the excellence of the story) was spasmodic. It may be noticed as a defect in *Familiar Studies of Men and Books* that no *character*, apart from traditional character, as in the case of Pepys, emerges from any of the essays: we are given accounts and criticisms of, for example, Burns; but we do not have them flashed out at us as real men. Stevenson, I think, had a very poor sense of character. In all these essays there is the same defect, an air of flatness, of colourlessness, such as we may find in any case where character has not been imagined.

Stevenson also required idiosyncrasy in a character before he could grasp it. There was for him no interest in normality of character, which somehow he did not grasp. Once he apprehended a personality all was different; then, every touch told, as we may see in the picture of old Weir, or even in Silver. If he grasped the character he could see it admirably; but it had to be "knobbly," for quiet, unpicturesque men baffled his powers of reproduction. He could admire, but he could not draw them. There is a very curious instance of this in the *Memoir of Fleeming Jenkin*, which is worth commenting on here. That memoir is in some ways perfunctory; as a whole it belongs to the same uncharacterised class of portrait-studies as these *Men and Books*. Jenkin is poorly drawn, so that he might be anybody. But there are passages in the *Memoir* which are the most moving passages that Stevenson ever wrote. They do not relate to Fleeming Jenkin, who is all out of focus: they relate to the parents of Jenkin and his wife. Jenkin's personality, it would seem, was never grasped by Stevenson; these vignettes, on the other hand, are quite poignantly real and quite pathetically beautiful.

VI

The characteristics of Stevenson's essays are in general, as I have tried to indicate, characteristics of manner rather than of matter. Happy notions for slight papers need not be detailed—there are many, which have in their time provoked great enthusiasm, and which will continue to give pleasure because they are a little whimsical in conception and very finished in performance. These essays owe their charm to the fact that Stevenson was often writing about himself, for he always wrote entertainingly about himself. He was charmed by himself, in a way that the common egoist has not the courage or possibly the imagination to be. Henley will tell you that Stevenson took every mirror into his confidence; an amusing and not at all distressing piece of vanity. His whole life was deliciously joined together by his naïve and attractive vanity. His essays, the most personal work of any he wrote, are filled with the same vanity which brought him (and kept him) such good friends. It was not the unhappy vanity that drives friends away, that is suspicious of all kindness: Stevenson had been too much petted as a child to permit of such wanton and morbid self-distrust. He was confident, but not vulgarly confident;

vain, to the extent of being more interested in himself than in anything else; but he was not dependent upon his earnings, and success came early enough to keep sweet his happy complacency. His essays show these things as clearly as do his letters. His essays "are like milestones upon the wayside of his life," and they are so obviously milestones, that all readers who are fascinated by autobiography, particularly if it be veiled, have been drawn to Stevenson as they are drawn to an attractive, laughing child. My own opinion is that Stevenson has sent his lovers away no richer than they came; but there are many who could not share that view, because there are many who are thankful to him for telling them that "it is better to be a fool than to be dead." I think Stevenson did not know what it was to be either a fool or dead. That state of nervous high spirits which is a part of his natural equipment for the battle, which lent even his most artificial writing a semblance of vivacity, prevented him from ever being dead (in the sense of supine or dull, as I suppose he meant it); and I cannot persuade myself that Stevenson was ever a fool.

It is for these reasons that I regard all such phrases in Stevenson's essays as pieces of purple, as things which, however they please some readers, are in themselves inherently false and artificial. That they were consciously false I do not believe. Stevenson, I am sure, had the phrase-making instinct: such a thing cannot be learned, as anyone may see by examining the work of merely imitative writers: it is a part of Stevenson's nature that he crystallised into a figure some obvious half-truth about life, and love, and fate, and the gimcrack relics of old heroisms. It is equally a part of his nature that he fell naturally into a sententious habit of moral utterance. Morality—as we may realise from the lengthy fragment called *Lay Morals*—preoccupied him. But it was morality expressed with the wagged head of sententious dogma. Finally, it comes to be true that, by whatever means, by whatever labour the art was attained, Stevenson was, above everything else, a writer. "There is no wonder," said Henley, in the notorious review of Mr. Graham Balfour's biography, "there is no wonder that Stevenson wrote his best in the shadow of the Shade; for writing his best was very life to him."

VII

As a writer, then, let Stevenson be regarded in the conclusion of this chapter upon his essays. As a theoretical writer he gives his deliberate example in that one essay *On some technical elements of Style in Literature* ; and his theories have aroused bitter comment. Because Stevenson found certain combinations of consonants recurrent in selected passages, it was assumed by his critics that he lived in a state of the dreariest kind of pattern-making. That, of course, was a mistake on the part of Stevenson's critics, because Stevenson was a prolific writer, and could never have afforded the time to be a mere hanger-on of words. What Stevenson did was first to realise that a prose style is not the result of accident. He saw that an evil use of adjective and over-emphasis weakened style; and he realised that a solved intricacy of sentence was part of the instinctive cunning by which a good writer lures readers to follow him with ever-growing interest into the most remote passages of his work. He was a careful writer, who revised with scrupulous care ; and some sentences of Stevenson, meandering most sweetly past their consonants and syllables and "knots," to their destined conclusion, are still, and I suppose always will be capable of yielding, a pure delight to the ear. Those who do not take Stevenson's pains will qualify his denunciation of the "natural" writer, because a natural writer is one whose ear is quick and fairly true: he is not necessarily producing "the disjointed babble of the chronicler," but he is incapable of the fine point of exquisite rhythm which we may find in Stevenson's best writing. That writing, various though it is (various, I mean, in "styles"), remains true to its musical principles. It is the result of trained ear and recognition of language as a conscious instrument. It has innumerable, most insidious appeals, to disregard which is a task for the barbarian. It is patterned, it is built of sounds,—"one sound suggests, echoes, demands, and harmonises with another,"—all in accordance with the expressed theory of Stevenson. We will grant it the delights, because they are incontestable. Let us now question whether it has not one grave defect.

All style which is so intricately patterned, so reliant upon its music, its rhythm, its balance, gratifies the ear in the way that old dance music gratifies the ear. The minuet and the saraband, stately as they are, have their slow phrases, and flow to their clear resolution with immemorial dignity; they are patterns of closely-woven figured style, than which we could hardly have an illustration more fit. They are examples of style less subtle than Stevenson's; but in Stevenson's writing there is no violence to old airs and the old order. His writing is only "a linkéd sweetness long drawn out," and in its differentiation from the old way of writing is to be found, not a revolution, not anarchy, but a weakness. Stevenson's style, graceful, sustained though it is, lacks power. It has finesse; but it has no vigour. The passages to which one turns are passages of delicious, stealthy accomplishment. They are passages which suggest the slow encroaching fingers of the in-coming tide, creeping and whispering further and further up the sand; and our watchful delight in the attainment of each sentence is the delight we feel in seeing the waves come very gently, pushed on by an incalculable necessity, until their length is reached and their substance is withdrawn. There is no tempestuous certainty in Stevenson's writing; there is not the magnificent wine of Shakespeare's prose, which has marvellous strength as well as its delicate precision. Stevenson's style, clearly invalidish in his imitators, has in itself the germs of their consumption. It is quiet, pretty, picturesque, graceful; it has figure and trope in plenty; but it has no vehemence. You may find in it an amazing variety of pitch and cadence; but at length the care that has made it betrays the artificer; at length the reader will look in vain for the rough word. That is the pity of Stevenson's style—not that he should have sought it, and exercised it, and made language quite the most important thing in his writing; but that his very artfulness should have yielded him no protection against the demand of nature for something which no care or cunning can ever put into style that does not carry its own impetus.

V

POEMS

I

The Scottish temperament is compounded of such various and unlikely ingredients that very many of those who charge Scots with hypocrisy and sentimentality are guilty of something like frigid intolerance. Hypocrisy, in the sense of self-deception, is too common a thing among all men to be charged particularly against the Scots; sentimentality, in the sense of false or artificially heightened emotion, is, in the same way, the prerogative of no particular nation or body of persons. It is very likely true that hypocrisy and sentimentality are among the failings of the Scots: but among their virtues may be found both integrity and sincerity as well as loyalty to an idea or to a conviction. What points the contradiction is that the Scots, in every meaning of that word, are very sensible. They are very clearly aware of all circumstances tending to their own advantage; they are very appreciative of good actions contributed by other persons to that advantage ; and they are very easily moved. They are easily moved by encounter, in unusual circumstances, with the Scots tongue (by which I mean that accent in speaking English, and those terms, grammatical or verbal, which are peculiar to Scotsmen) ; and they are extraordinarily moved by the word "home," by the thought of family and by certain sounds, such as music heard across water, or particular notes in the voice of a singer—especially when the singer happens to be the person who is moved. But they are not singular in these susceptibilities, although they may provide a notorious example of them. In each case the emotion is easy, sympathetic, instantaneous ; in each case it takes the form of tears. Those who cry are, as it were, drunken with a certain impulse of humility ; they may be as distressing as a drunken person grown maudlin ; but, superficial though it is, their emotion is entirely genuine. It is of no use to call it sentimentality : it is simply objectless emotion, which may not be very stirring to those who do not feel it, but which is not therefore to be instantly condemned. It happens to be a tradition that Englishmen do not publicly show affection or weep : how hard it is that we should weigh in the balance of our own traditions the practices of our neighbours!

This point, however, is a most interesting one, because it helps to explain the dearth of great Scottish poets, and because it helps to explain why, in spite of every good intention, Stevenson never made any impression upon English readers by his three volumes of miscellaneous "grown-up" poetry. The fault was not a personal one; but was a part of the national character. The Scots are so easily moved, and their tears and enthusiasms flow so freely, that the authenticity of tears and enthusiasms is even disputed, and the power to go deeper is not vouchsafed them. They appear to us, as the Master of Ballantrae appeared to Ephraim Mackellar, compounded of "outer sensibility and inner toughness"; and Burns, the only great Scottish poet, triumphed because these constituents were granted to him in more overflowing and undiluted measure than has been the case with any other Scotsman. Outer sensibility and inner toughness is a phrase that would label a good many Englishmen; but of Englishmen the mixture makes charlatans, whereas of Scotsmen it makes journalists and novelists and lawyers of extraordinary skill and astonishing industry. That is why it seems to me important that we should be slow to charge a race that is impressionable with the insincerity (conscious or unconscious) which we might suspect in individual Englishmen. The failure of a Scotsman to be a great poet is another matter.

II

Stevenson's poems are contained in four small volumes—*Underwoods*, *Ballads*, *Songs of Travel* (a collection made by himself, but published posthumously), and *A Child's Garden of Verses*. Of the four volumes the one that has enjoyed most popularity, as well as most critical esteem, is *A Child's Garden of Verses*, which book, although, by Stevenson's account, very easily produced, has the value of being unique in scheme and contents. The other volumes have less in them of wide interest, and so they are less generally read. Certain poems, such as the *Requiem* ("Under the wide and starry sky") and *The Vagabond* ("Give to me the life I love") arise whenever the name of Stevenson is fondly mentioned; they are, as it were, the stock-in-trade of the conversational anthologist, who, in the same spirit, will have suggested to him by the name of Meredith the words, "Enter these enchanted woods, Ye who dare." These two poems are not the best poems Stevenson wrote; but they are handy for remembrance. That explains their frequent employment; that, and their appropriateness to the conventional idea of Stevenson, which is based upon a sentimental and mediocre marvel at the unconventionality of the open road.

The best poems Stevenson wrote are his ballads. With a story to tell, he was keener to represent truly the subject-matter upon which he was engaged; and this engendered the "heat of composition," if it did not always spring from the native heat or intensity of inspiration. The ballads, especially *Ticonderoga*, have a swift effectiveness and an adherence to theme which is not so marked in the poems provoked by occasional events. In these the rhyme and form sometimes lead the way, and the poems become exercises in friendly versification, without much feeling, and with only that Scottish affectionateness to which reference has already been made. Examples of impoverished emotion may be found in the two poems expressing gladness at visits from Mr. Henry James. As cheerful little outbursts of pleasure, such poems, in manuscript, would be interesting, even delightful: as poems they fall short of complete success, even in their own class, for the reason that they are as conversational and as fluent as Stevenson's letters, and are diffuse as his prose rarely is.

Better than these are some of the dryly humorous Scots dialect poems, such as *The Spaewife*, with its refrain of "*—It's gey an' easy spierin'*, says the beggar-wife to me." These again are often purely experimental versifications; but they are more than the casual rhymings of the pleased householder, and they have more interest as poetry. Far and away better even than these, however, because it is the expression of a personal and, I think, a deep feeling, is that poem, included in *Songs of Travel*, and quoted in *The Master of Ballantrae*, which is untitled, but which is written "To the tune of Wandering Willie."

> "Home no more home to me, whither must I wander?
> Hunger my driver, I go where I must."

In this poem there seems to be real emotion, as I think there is in the dedication to Mrs. Stevenson of *Weir of Hermiston*. In other poems there is a grace and the mellifluous flow of words which Stevenson could always command; but the verses make a pattern, and a pattern of only occasional significance. They are thus robbed of any power to move us æsthetically.

The two long narrative poems, *The Ballad of Rahero* and *The Feast of Famine*, are both well-sustained by a body of incident. They have, in lieu of emotion, a certain vividness of excitement. One is excited by what is going forward, one must read on for the story. In the degree, therefore, in which one's attention is removed from the versification, these two narratives are good; and those other verses based on legends—*Heather Ale* and *Ticonderoga*—would be sufficient to emphasise the fact that Stevenson loved a story and was always at his best with a tale to spin. When, however, we reach poems in which no story is to be told, we are confronted with an absence of emotion which robs the pages we read of all that exceeds mere pleasurable line-scanning. Happy lines there are, turns of phrase that perhaps have given rise to the poem into which they are woven. But they are only, at best, the amiable pleasantries of one who could handle with dexterity the words of whose music his mind was full. "The bright ring of words" is not the phrase of a poet; it is the phrase of a connoisseur, and of one who used words as a connoisseur uses them. The poet is a singer first: he does not make a poem out of his craft. And the tendency to diffuseness which mars many of the longer lyrics is a curious instance of failure in a writer who regarded compression as an essential of good style.

POEMS

III

In *A Child's Garden of Verses* Stevenson was doing a thing which had never really been done before. There are nursery rhymes which crystallise children's ideas; but this book actually shows, in what we must believe to be an extraordinarily happy way, the working of a particular child mind over a great variety of matters. Its excellence is due to the fact that Stevenson's young days, lonely as some of them had been, had never lacked interest, had always been full of those simple and direct pleasures of incident and encounter and memory which happy children enjoy. The world had been full of a number of things; and the memory of those things had abided. It was the memory of a fanciful rather than an imaginative childhood, a childhood of superstitions and sports, of a buried tin soldier and of the pleasant land of play; but we must not forget that such poems as *My Treasures*, poor in some of their lines, are finely imaginative reconstructions, the naïveté of which prevents many readers from estimating their quality. So with *The Unseen Playmate*, which, although it is a poem for grown-ups, reveals an understanding of a most important fact in children's games far more profound than are the pretentious and unconvincing lines to R. A. M. Stevenson in *Underwoods*. Even if the idea of *The Unseen Playmate* may be the idea of a grown-up pretending, the writing of this, as of the other verses, is almost without lapse, charmingly simple and natural. I believe it is a fact that children appreciate and even delight in *A Child's Garden of Verses*, not merely at the bidding of their parents, but as a normal manifestation of taste. This in itself would be a proof that the book is already a secondary nursery classic. For our present purpose, if that does not seem rather an overbearing way of valuing a book so slight in form, it is sufficient to say that Stevenson's success here was due to the fact that he was legitimately using the memory of actual experience. Too many of his serious, or grown-up, poems show their models; too many of them flow undistinguished by any truly poetic quality; too many of them are experiments in metre or rhyme, such as one may write for fun, but never for free circulation. *The Child's Garden of Verses* alone, then, of the four volumes, exhibits a strict harmony of design with performance. Its dedication to Stevenson's nurse, Alison Cunningham, serves only to make the book more complete.

IV

Implicit in the strictures upon Stevenson's poetry which have preceded this paragraph is the assumption that Milton's requirements of poetry—that it should be simple, sensuous, passionate—is fundamentally true as applied to lyrical poetry. It would be troublesome to apply such a test to many of the minor poets; and it may be that a few of Stevenson's poems would stand the test. Not many of them, however, because none of them shows a depth of emotion uncommon to the ordinarily sensitive person. Stevenson was sensitive to many things; without sensitiveness he could not have written *A Child's Garden of Verses* or that very excellent ballad *Ticonderoga*. But sensitiveness is only a poor substitute for emotion; and Stevenson's emotion ran in the few ordinary channels of the normal Scotsman. He loved home; he loved those around him; he desired to be loved, to be free of the fear of poverty, to live in comfort and in health. Those things he felt deeply, as Scotsmen, as most men, do. He loved truth; but it was a conventional truth; a truth, that is to say, improvised from ordinary usage, from hearsay, from the dogma of "that station of life"; a truth such as any man who finds himself born in a little pit of earth may harden his moral shell and his imagination and stultify his spiritual curiosity by accepting; and it was a truth out of which Stevenson was escaping towards the end of his life. But in all this love of virtues and duties and usages there was never until Stevenson's emergence into the greater freedom of life in the South Seas the passionate love of anything for its own sake. If he loved the open air it was with a pleasant, "playing" love, a sort of self-indulgence. Over his heart he kept the watchful guard of a Protestant Scotsman. It was unmoved, a secret, not to be known. It did not inform his work, in which there is sometimes a heat of composition, or even a heat of feeling, but never the cold heat of profound and piercing emotion. That he was capable of being easily moved, that he loved virtue and hated cruelty and wrong, these things are true. That he could grow hot at a calumny, as he did in the defence of Father Damien, is equally true. But these things are the signs of a prudent man, eagerly interested in life, rather taking pleasure in the thought that he is hot to attack injustice; not of a profound thinker or of a poet. They warm us with, perhaps, affection for Stevenson; they keep alive our admiration for him as an attractive figure in our literary history. They do not thrill us, because they appeal to the interest and excitement and honesty and feeling in us, and not to those more secret, more passionate reserves which we yield only to the poet.

VI

PLAYS

I

It is a commonplace of dramatic reporting, which in spite of its frequently doubtful application has the truth of an old saw, that the novelist cannot write plays. Certainly, it would seem that the qualities which go to the making of good plays are not precisely those which make good novels ; for while it is possible to conceive a novel in terms of narrative, descriptions of abounding nature, psychological analysis, and tableaux, the play has rules more strictly objective and more definitely rigid. Now if we, for the moment, pass over the question of Stevenson's collaborator in the four printed plays with which his name is associated, and if we, for this occasion, treat them as though they were his work entirely, we shall be better able to distinguish certain remarkable characteristics of these plays, and, anticipating certain general conclusions to be made later, of Stevenson's talent.

PLAYS

Stevenson, we are all aware, was never, strictly speaking, in spite of *Catriona* and *Weir of Hermiston*, a novelist. He was a writer of many kinds of stories; but they were not primarily, until we come to *Weir*, domestic or psychological. Many of them were what no doubt would commonly be called "dramatic," in the sense that they contained scenes of some violence; but for the most part they were narrative interspersed with tableaux. They were "picturesque," not because they were startlingly visual, but because Stevenson had that *flair* for the odd, the startling, or the vivid effect of contrast which is generally described by the word "picturesque." It was the oddness of *Dr. Jekyll and Mr. Hyde* that allured him before he became oppressed by its symbolism. It was, equally, oddness that always attracted him in character: he had no profound sense of character, for this reason. Passivity he never understood. His characters must forever be in action. That, it might be supposed, was in itself a first reason for turning to the theatre, since, according to modern dramatic reporters, "drama" is a word synonymous with the word "action." Action, something doing—that, by the recipe, is the certain play. But while action may give a play breathless suspense, while it may provide the kind of play which, in a specifically theatrical sense, is called a "drama," action is not the whole battle. To action, or at least to the psychological excitement created by a sense of action in progress and a climax pending, must be added a very powerful sense of what is effective in the theatre. A pause, a sound, verbal repetition, an abrupt change—these things are crude examples, chosen at random from among the obvious instances of what contributes to the sense of the theatre. If we think of such things as the tapping of Pew's stick (in *Admiral Guinea*), and, in *Deacon Brodie*, the appearance of the masked Deacon at the window by which Leslie is watching for him, we shall realise that in some degree, in some very obvious and primitive form, Stevenson was possessed of this attribute. But one thing we shall infallibly discover him to lack, a thing which Mr. Henry James missed in *Catriona*, a thing which has vital importance in drama—the visual sense. These plays show no real power of visualising a scene. Picturesque they all are; they all have qualities which make them engrossing—as reading. But they are not focussed for the eyes, and they are not well constructed for real dramatic effect.

Deacon Brodie is in five acts and eight

tableaux, and its effects are indescribably broken, so that irrelevancies are numerous, distracting side-issues over-emphasised, and so that the Deacon is almost a minor character. It is hard to realise that there are only a dozen persons in the play, for their comings and goings are so frequent as to give the effect of a confused number of straggling participants in desultory action. The play itself centres round an historical figure—Deacon Brodie—who was an honest man before the world by day, and by night an expert cracksman. His name is familiar both in criminal history and in the annals of Edinburgh, where his activities became, after his death, notorious. In the play, Brodie at last is eager for reform; but one of his cronies, tempted by a Bow Street runner, and the only one of Brodie's friends to yield to temptation, betrays him. Though Brodie escapes, his absence from home has been discovered in the excitement consequent upon his father's death, and, when arrest is imminent, he takes his own life. Stevenson had found the details of Brodie's life while he was preparing the sketches collected under the title *Edinburgh: Picturesque Notes*; and it is conceivable that in some measure the play's technique was a little influenced by a reading of some eighteenth-century episodic plays, such, for example, as Gay's "Beggar's Opera," which is similarly broken in construction, though more permissibly so, because "The Beggar's Opera" is no more than a skein in which ballads and satire may be found to provide our entertainment. This mention of "The Beggar's Opera" must not be taken too seriously, however, because although that play deals with the life of highwaymen and pickpurses and thief-takers in the eighteenth century, as *Deacon Brodie* does, it is profoundly real, whereas *Deacon Brodie* is only too obviously modern fake. Macheath and Polly Peachum are infinitely more real than Brodie and his doxy. Moreover the ensemble in *Deacon Brodie* is on the whole poorly conceived. The minor persons are mere figures, introduced to stand here or there, or do this or that, and are labelled with names and idiosyncrasies. The major persons, though more detailed, have an equal lack of vitality. It is necessary to add the further explanation that *Deacon Brodie* is the first of the plays, and that it dates from 1880. It is easily the least coherent of them all. Stevenson was to improve upon *Deacon Brodie* in that respect, at least.

II

The two lightest plays—*Beau Austin* and *Macaire*—are experiments, the one in manner, the other in bizarre or, as it is styled by the authors, "melodramatic farce." The manner of *Beau Austin* is the manner of the costume play. It is highly sophisticated, and its key-note is powder and patches. The beau is at his toilet, and one of the women he has betrayed is in the town, still sick with despair at her soiled virtue. Her true love hears from the lady's lips the story of her betrayal, and, on being forbidden to challenge the beau, contents himself with demanding a marriage ceremony. His flatteries are effective, the beau consents, and the formal proposal is made, only to be rejected by the lady, whose hauteur is aroused. So matters stand when the lady's brother, learning by chance of the betrayal, insults the beau before an important personage. As climax, the beau proposes publicly, and is as publicly accepted. It will be seen that the play could not claim, excepting in respect of verbal artifice, to be more than a pretty jig-saw. It could have no effect of reality: the effect desired by the authors was one purely of the stage. Verbally it is exquisitely dexterous. That is its undoing.

The attempt is made to convey in words something more than the action of the piece would successfully carry: words are to create an atmosphere of the eighteenth century fashionable life, to indicate the possibility that calm picturesque heartless exteriors shielded even then hearts that beat warmly beneath lace and brocade. The play was a pretence that nothing was something, a pretty moving picture under the perception of which, beating out in pianissimo airs from appropriate music, and the faint throb of an unseen minuet, was the delicate heart of the period. It was an æsthetic view of the eighteenth century, the century of Fielding and of Smollett, tinkered about to make a perpetual *bal masque*, or, shall we say, a picture by Watteau or Fragonard. In point of fact the play is too slight to bear its weight of intention: it remains verbal. As drama it is more negligible than "Monsieur Beaucaire" or "The Adventure of Lady Ursula," because its literary pretensions are so much more elaborate. It has sometimes fine shades of close verbal fence that are Meredithian: it is better to read than it could be to see. But it is an attempt, one might say an almost basely cunning attempt, to capture the theatre as a place where costumes grace a barren play. It failed because its authors were two conscientious literary men, bent upon a superficial perfection undreamed of by practical dramatists. Just as Cowper, in translating Homer, made an epic for a tea-party, so Henley and Stevenson made about the rational and cynical eighteenth century a sophisticated play for a boudoir. They concentrated upon the superficial, and only said, but did not show, that the men and women of the eighteenth century had hearts as true and passionate as those of our day. The play lacked realism, and, more disastrously, it lacked reality.

On the other hand, *Macaire* has a thin air of jocularity which almost carries it through. It has a sententious cleric, a drunken notary, a repetitious father for the bride, a courteous host, a little mystery of the bridegroom's nurseling days, the facetious Macaire and his companion. It has all these things, and it has an idea, strong enough for a single act, stretched to its thinnest over several acts which demand cuts more severe than the authors allow.

Macaire escaping from justice, threatened each moment, in the face of the audience, with instant arrest, carries himself with unfailing *sang-froid* through all his difficulties but the last. Finding a chance of sport, and possibly of profit, he impersonates an erring father. The real father appears. Macaire still, after the manner of Mr. Jingle, is imperturbable. Competition follows, until the desire for the genuine father's money becomes too strong for Macaire. Then only does he show the blackness of his heart, which does not shrink, in such desperate situations, from murder. So Macaire, still talking, still watchful and unscrupulous, is brought to bay. Fiercely turning, in a picturesque situation, upon the stairs, he is shot by a gendarme on the stage. That is a skeleton of the play; but the play is again a literary play, so that sensationalism will not redeem it. By repetitions of catch-phrases and by trivial incidents which (e.g. the exchanging of the wine-bottles) are not unknown to the humbler kinds of drama, the story is continued until its idle joking can no longer be suddenly stirred into flaming melodrama by the noise and zest of bloody crime. It has many shrewd bids for theatrical effectiveness; but it faints for want of a fabric upon which its devices might flourish and triumphantly justify themselves.

III

The fourth play, *Admiral Guinea*, has fine qualities, both literary and dramatic; it is the least literary and the most dramatically effective of all the plays. It contains one figure, in Pew, which might have been, as far as one may judge in reading, a hauntingly gruesome object; and, in spite of Stevenson's own subsequent contempt for this play and for *Macaire*, shows a greater, if conventional, power of simplification than does any of the other plays. Admiral Guinea, a retired and penitent slaver, refuses his daughter her lover, on the ground that the lover is ungodly. Pew, an old associate of Admiral Guinea, become blind for his sins, and still full of vengeful wickedness, arrives in the neighbourhood, catches the lover drunk, leads him back to Admiral Guinea's cottage, and tries, with his aid, to rob his old captain of certain riches which he supposes to lie in a brass-bound chest. The young man's reaction, their discovery by Admiral Guinea, the violent death of the unrepentant Pew follow; whereupon the lovers are suitably blessed by Admiral Guinea.

It has been said, above, that this play shows a greater power of simplification than the others; the action of it is certainly quicker, more obvious, less choked with verbal expressiveness, than is the action of the other plays; and in so far as this is so it would appear that *Admiral Guinea* is a considerable advance, technically, upon them.

The simplification is, to some considerable extent, effected by a strange poverty of invention, and the play is likest of all to those nondescripts which Stevenson as a little boy must have performed upon his toy stage, with paper figures pushed hither and thither in tin slides upon the boards. In spite of that, *Admiral Guinea* is the best of the plays because, in a higher degree than its fellows, it is truly actable. We cannot regard the confused cramped episodic *Deacon Brodie* as theatrically effective. Equally it is impossible, from the standpoint of public performance, to consider as satisfactory either *Beau Austin* or *Macaire*. *Admiral Guinea*, however, even if it belongs to a class of play which is associated in our minds with such titles as "Black-Eyed Susan," has its action very largely comprised in the material put upon the stage; it has the obvious stage effects of darkness and the dreadful tapping stick of Pew; and it has picturesque struggles, death, wounded and reasserted honour, and, for these plays, a minimum of soliloquy. More it would be impossible to claim for *Admiral Guinea* without seeing it performed: again we have types roughly "mannered" to serve as persons of the play: but they are types clearly in accordance with tradition, and they preserve their interest fully until they are done with and put away with the footlight-wicks, and the tin slides, and the other paraphernalia of the toy stage—paper figures, a penny plain, and twopence coloured.

IV

For that brings us to the pathetic final explanation of the failure of the Henley-Stevenson plays. We may say that they are deficient in drama, or that they are trivial in theme, or that they have no visual sense to illumine them for our eyes; but the truth is that they fail because they are false. The theatre has in it much that is false. much to which we deliberately shut our eyes in order that we may accept the dramatist's formal conventions. We do not, in the theatre, demand that "King Lear" shall be accompanied by a pandemonium of crackling tin and iron and artificial whoopings of wind. Those things we prefer to imagine for ourselves. But somehow the mixture of legitimate convention and the basest imitation of reality has been confused in the theatre. The exaggeration regarded as necessary by an effete system of acting and production has created other unpardonable falsenesses. The stage has been a place upon which actors disported themselves. It was of such a stage that Stevenson thought. In each case he hung a play upon a sensational figure—Brodie, Macaire, Pew, and, in a much lesser degree, upon the picturesque figure of Beau Austin. To him the drama was nothing but play. It was an excuse—nay, a demand, for unreality. He supposed that stage characters really were cardboard figures such as he had known, moralising ranters, virtuous girls, spouters of Latin tags, pious brands from the burning, handsome courageous puppet-like juvenile leads, and so on. It never occurred to him to put a real figure in a play: he never supposed that a character in a play had any end but to be put back in the box with the other playthings. That is really the cause of the shallowness of these four plays. As Stevenson admitted to Mr. Henry James, he heard people talking, and felt them acting, and that seemed to him to be fiction. But to hear people talking and to feel them acting bespeaks a very unmaterial conception of them: if a character in a play talks, however monotonously, without developing any personality save that of verbal mannerism, we are bound to feel that he has not been realised. And just as Stevenson realised none of the characters in his plays, so we are powerless to realise them. We find them, as Professor Saintsbury pathetically found Catriona herself, bloodless. Professor Saintsbury found Catriona full of sawdust, while of thc characters in the plays we have used the word "paper": very well, the impression of lifelessness is as clearly felt in each case. And such an impression, carried to its logical end, explains why, in at least one department of letters, Stevenson from the first mistook his ground. Not one of the four plays has serious value as an example of dramatic art; it is clear that not one of them so far has commended itself to the public or to the actor-managers. Yet the plays were obviously set to catch the popular taste, and their literary finish, a confession in itself of an absence of dramatic impulse, does not succeed in commending them to those who judge by more exacting standards.

VII

SHORT STORIES

I

STEVENSON himself establishes the fact that he found short-story writing easier than the writing of novels. "It is the length that kills," he confessed. But length offered difficulties in the longer stories because Stevenson, besides lacking the physical endurance for continuous imaginative effort, had the experimental and inventive mind rather than the synthetic or the analytical. It was easier for him to see the whole of a short story. It could be compressed: it had not to be sustained. And in the writing of a short story his confidence never slackened. He was then not sailing in uncharted seas. It is for this reason, in the first place, that Stevenson's short stories are better as works of art than his long ones. A little idea, a flash, it may be, of inspiration; and Stevenson had his story complete, ready for that scrupulous handling and manipulation which the actual composition always involved.

He did not greatly deal in anecdote; his psychological studies are inclined to be hollow; but he was perfectly effective in his not very powerful vein of fantasy, could tell a fairy tale with distinction, succeeded once without question in picturesque drama, and, when he fell to anecdote, as in *The Treasure of Franchard*, *Providence and the Guitar*, and *The Beach of Falesá*, he was pleasantly triumphant. Moreover, in two of his "bogle" stories, the one inserted in *Catriona*, and the other famous to all the world as *Thrawn Janet*, he seems to me to have risen clearly above anecdote with matter which might have been left as unsatisfactory as it remains in *The Body-Snatcher*.

In one of his reviews Stevenson speaks of "that compression which is the mark of a really sovereign style." Compression is no more the mark of a sovereign style, of course, than it is of a suit of clothes. Compression brings with it obscurity, and is a mark of self-consciousness. What Stevenson meant was possibly a justification of apophthegm and figure. He rather enjoyed what somebody once called "minting the arresting phrase." There is, at any rate, a palpable connection between our two quotations. But it is certain that precision, austerity, or, if I may use the word, chastity, of expression is a sign of good style;

and compression, where it takes the form of heightening and intensification of effect, is the mark of a good short story. It is the mark of Stevenson's best stories. It is the mark of *Thrawn Janet*, of *The Pavilion on the Links*, of *The Bottle Imp*. Sometimes, after promising well, Stevenson abandons himself, it is true, to his natural Scottish aptitude, and literally "talks out" such tales as *Markheim* and *A Lodging for the Night*; but, quite as often, his judgment beats his inclination, and the result is a classic short story in a language not too brilliantly equipped with examples of the craft.

For the short story is above all a matter of *justesse*, by which word I mean to suggest delicate propriety of expression to idea. Mr. Henry James can tell a short story, because Mr. Henry James writes, as it were, with a very fine pen. Stevenson was not comparable as an artist with Mr. Henry James; but he wrote in a less rarified atmosphere; and it is still practically an unsettled question whether a distinguished artist (one who perfectly expresses a fine conception), such as Turgenev or Mr. Henry James, is the superior or the inferior of the writer with more tumultuous sympathies whose sense of form is less than his sense of life. So that when Stevenson wrote *The Pavilion on the Links*, or *The Bottle Imp*, or *Thrawn Janet*, or *Markheim*, he was writing particular stories of which only the last, one supposes, could ever have occurred to Mr. James as a subject for a short story at all. Conversely, one sees Stevenson blundering into the bluntnesses and certainly the ultimate failure of *Olalla*, with the knowledge that his delicacy of style was more marked than the poignancy of his perception; and the psychological explorations of *Olalla* are jejune stumblings compared with the finished delicacy of "Washington Square." One does not think, in reading, of Mr. James; but one may perhaps be permitted to illustrate a point by a reference to his work, which has no precise significance as a parallel. That fact, I hope, will excuse a momentary comparison for the purpose of showing that *Will o' the Mill*, for all its stylistic accomplishment, is a barren piece of moralising. Where Stevenson essayed profundity, as all writers are drawn to essay profundity, whether it is from natural profoundness or from the instinct of imitation, he was badly hampered by his inexperience as an inductive philosopher. Both *Will o' the Mill* and *Markheim* are, as it were, appendages to that doleful failure *Prince Otto*. They were experiments for Stevenson in a particular genre for which talent and his mental training had lent him no aptitude. It was on other work that he more successfully took his stand as a writer of short stories. His success—considering that we are now examining his position among the masters of our literature—can only be attested where his work stands supreme or, at any rate, is clearly distinguished, in its own class. It cannot be doubted for one moment that Stevenson wrote some exceedingly fine short stories, fit to be compared, in their own line, with any that have been written in English. What follows must be read in the light of this claim. In their own way, I regard *The Suicide Club*, *The Pavilion on the Links*, *Providence and the Guitar*, *Thrawn Janet*, *The Treasure of Franchard*, *The Beach of Falesá*, and *The Bottle Imp* as first-class short stories. In a distinct second class I should place *The Rajah's Diamond*, some of *The Dynamiter* stories, *The Merry Men*, *Will o' the Mill*, *Markheim*, *Olalla*, *The Isle of Voices*, and *Dr. Jekyll and Mr. Hyde*. The least successful short stories seem to me to be *The Story of a Lie*, *A Lodging for the Night*, *The Sire de Malétroit's Door*, *The Misadventures of John Nicholson*, and *The Body-Snatcher*. I am aware that one at least of the stories which I have placed in this third division—*The Sire de Malétroit's Door*—has given great pleasure to many readers, and has even been not without its direct influence upon Stevenson's imitators, while another—*A Lodging for the Night*—is greatly admired, and has been very highly praised; so that it seems hardly necessary to say that the classification is roughly made, and that it is only here attempted for reasons of convenience. The stories will hereafter be grouped according to subject or treatment, and will be examined individually. Those in the first division are, I think, completely successful in their own conventions; those in the second division are either incompletely successful or successful in conventions which seem to me inferior in artistic value; those in the third division are, as far as I can see, unsuccessful either because they fail to impose their conventions upon the reader or because they fail to convince the reader that Stevenson had mastered the craft of short-story writing. But, upon the whole, I believe Stevenson's short stories to represent more successfully than any other part of his output the variety and the brilliance of his talent. It is for this reason that I shall endeavour in some detail to justify the divisions indicated above, and to emphasise the fact that such tentative distinctions, even if they prove inaccurate in the case of some one or two stories, may yet have some value as providing a basis for agreement or disagreement.

II

For that reason I shall add that the stories in the third division seem to me to fail for these reasons. *The Story of a Lie* is obviously prentice work. It is presumably based upon some experience of his own in France; but the action, once transferred from the Continent, is filled with sentimentality. Although written, apparently, much later than *The Story of a Lie*, *The Misadventures of John Nicholson* is a protracted anecdote which does not awaken very much interest by its attempt to blend humorous exaggeration with bizarre incidents. *The Body-Snatcher* is one which Stevenson had to supply in order to satisfy a journal with which he had made a contract. It is meant to shock us, but it loses power before the climax, which thereupon fails to shock. The idea is horrible, and affords scope for much dreadful detail: Stevenson, however, perhaps through ill-health, was unsuccessful with it, and possibly the ugliness of the whole thing is at fault. For *The Sire de Malétroit's Door* I must confess to the greatest distaste. It seems to me to have neither historical nor human convincingness; and the phrase at the end of the story, "her falling body" very significantly conveys the pin-cushion substance of the demoiselle whose indiscretion gives rise to the sickly and cloying tale. The last story in this division is one that enjoys great reputation, first because it deals with Villon, second because there is an outburst of Villon's against the red hair of a murdered man, and last because there is an elaborately written but entirely inconclusive duologue between Villon and his host. The story seems to me to be without point or form.

I believe that popular admiration for *A Lodging for the Night* is largely founded upon tradition or imitation, like the popular admiration for Shakespeare, without the basis of fact upon which the popular admiration for Shakespeare rests. It is well known that popular appreciation of great things is shallow, and that it rises from a common attempt to emulate the enthusiasm of the apostles of Art. Unfortunately, popular appreciation is more easily aroused by artifice than by art. Accordingly, those who have been taught to cite "Put out the light, and then—Put out the light" as a profundity are ready to cite with equal conviction the saying of Villon in this story that the murdered man had no right to have red hair. It is one of those dreadful æsthetic blunders that quickly pass into unquestionable dogma. If no protest is made, if those who detect an imposture remain supine, the false continues to masquerade as the magnificent ; and common opinions are so impervious to proclaimed fact that it is at length impossible to cope with them, save by some such wearisome exposition as this. It should be remembered that common appreciation of art is not guided by principles but by intuitions and imitations. The decay of a thing once widely popular is slow ; and it is due, not to any native perception of mistake, but to the sluggard realisation that the old enthusiasm is less ardently canvassed than it was. *A Lodging for the Night* has enjoyed great repute, because Stevenson " found " Villon at a time when other young men were finding Villon ; and now that Villon is quite settled among the young men, Stevenson's essay on Villon and his story about Villon have reached the larger public that is always some years after the fleeting fashion. The result is that, by imitation of those who ought to have known better, and even by its muddled acceptance of a bad play about Villon (called " If I were King "), the public has been led to esteem *A Lodging for the Night* as something more than the piece of laboured artifice that it always was.

In the second class I believe that *The Rajah's Diamond*, *The Dynamiter*, and *Dr. Jekyll and Mr. Hyde* are very efficient pieces of craftsmanship, strong enough in invention to delight that typical person called by Mr. H. G. Wells the "weary giant," engrossing reading to the accompaniment of cigars and whisky-and-soda, but not, in the way of art, quite what we require from works of creative imagination. *The Merry Men*, with one striking piece of characterisation, has vigour, but poor form and several superfluities of invention. *The Isle of Voices* is a pleasant enough fairy-tale, but clearly inferior to its companion piece *The Bottle Imp*. The other three tales, *Will o' the Mill*, *Markheim*, and *Olalla* are all psychological studies of a kind that is nowadays called arid. That is to say, they have greater elaborateness of treatment than their intrinsic importance quite justifies. *Will o' the Mill* is written with great softness and delicacy, in a sort of slow and lulling drone very sweet to the ear; *Markheim* has great virtuosity, is faint and exquisite in manner, feeble in perception, and is sometimes, I believe, false in psychology. Its plan and its manner would only be finally true if its understanding pierced more sharply and finely to the heart of truth. It lacks penetration. *Olalla* is, in many ways, fine, in some, beautiful. It is, however, as Stevenson came to be aware, false. It is false, not because it is insincere, but because Stevenson's knowledge had not the temper and the needle-like capacity to go ever deeper into the subtleties upon which he was engaged. I suspect that he dared not trust his imagination, that his imagination had more ingenuity than courage or strength. The story does not produce æsthetic emotion : it is as though the author had made a fine net to trap a moonbeam, as though, when he thought to have come at the heart of the matter, it had escaped him. He was perhaps not wise enough in the mysteries of the human soul. Sensitiveness, and the desire to create a passionate beauty, were not fit substitutes for that patient and courageous, that fearless imagination which alone could have given truth to so simple and so unseizable a problem. More, in his handling of the conclusion of his tale, Stevenson's emotion fell to a lower plane, and his talent played him quite false. He became too intent upon his *rendering* of the idea ; his literary sense took command when his knowledge failed. That is the weakness of all these three stories.

III

Finally, in the first division, we have seven stories. *Providence and the Guitar* and *The Treasure of Franchard* are what we may call, if we wish to do so, sentimental stories. Both are comedies of light character, both show certain influences ; but to both the manner, tender and amused, is so appropriate that we are pleased as we were meant to be pleased. Both contain good characterisation and an unstrained knowledge. Both are so entirely naïve in conception that we do not question the inspiration by which they were produced. In style and character dissimilar, but in humour of a like kind, are *The Suicide Club* and *The Bottle Imp*. These four stories are all marked with the whimsical and charming manner which made Stevenson so many friends in life. All are more or less lifted by fantasy above their common play with the humours and the pathos of daily affairs. They are founded upon Stevenson's natural attitude—*The Suicide Club*, more convincingly than *The Superfluous Mansion*, in which story the idea appears in its native ingenuousness, is an example of Stevenson's constant wish (a wish not unshared by others) that he might be singled out mysteriously by the agent for some strange adventure in the manner of "The White Cat." The young man in *The Superfluous Mansion*, it will be remembered, was thrilled by an invitation to enter a carriage in which a solitary lady sat : his adventure thereafter was more commonplace, for Stevenson's wish had in fact gone no further than the invitation to the carriage. So Prince Florizel embodied a desire for strange safe experience, such as all lonely children feel; and Stevenson was as much gratified as we are at the adventure of the young man with the cream tarts. My own opinion is, that it was the young man with the cream tarts who mattered; and that in the subsequent intrigues the story falls away to the level of *The Rajah's Diamond.* To be accosted by a young man with cream tarts in a locality so picturesque as Leicester Square—that is romance: to go to the suicide club, and to participate in what follows, is to leave romance for picturesque stimulation of interest by bizarre incident. The young man, I think, is art: the rest might have been invented by a person without imagination, and so we might call it craft. Nevertheless, even if the events subsequent to the young man with the cream tarts take on a more commonplace air, they have yet an individuality above that of the tales in *The Rajah's Diamond,* and the peculiar fantastic bravado of Stevenson's writing maintains the quality of surprise with extreme gusto. *The Bottle Imp* is, to me, comparable in quality with *Thrawn Janet* alone; and these two stories offer the two most successful examples of Stevenson's art as a short-story writer. Each in its way is perfect, in form and in manner. *The Beach of Falesá*, more anecdotal, and less fine in form than any of the other stories in this division, has excellences of character, emotion, and reality which may elsewhere be considered to be lacking. In all its details it is possibly more vital and more worth the telling than *The Pavilion on the Links*, which in form is superior, but which, in convention, is inferior. I know of nothing with which to compare *The Beach of Falesá*; and *The Pavilion on the Links* is perhaps not wholly outside the range of so accomplished a craftsman as Sir Arthur Conan Doyle, or so determined a romancer as Sir Arthur Quiller-Couch. That may be so, and very likely both those gentlemen admire *The Pavilion on the Links* very much. The fact that requires to be recorded here of this story is that it sustains its own note magnificently; and that if we grant this type of story the right to be described as art *The Pavilion on the Links* is the best example of the type known to us. It is continuously exciting; it is not oppressively false; and it is handled with extreme competence. Possibly one admires its craftsmanship, its consummate treatment of a theme from whose reality one withdraws one's conviction when the story's grip has relaxed, more than one admires its quality as a work of imagination. If that is so, one must certainly regard *The Pavilion on the Links* as a magnificent example of craft, but on a lower artistic plane than Stevenson's best work.

That brings to an end our consideration of the three rough divisions formulated at the beginning of this chapter. It is possible now to group the stories into their particular kinds, and to attempt to obtain, from an examination of these, some more general estimate of Stevenson's ability as a writer of short stories. As a preliminary to this it will be desirable to set forth what may be regarded as a principle of judgment; and then to tabulate the stories in their various kinds. Thus we shall be able to eliminate the inferior stories, and to arrive at certain, I hope reasonable, conclusions as to the place occupied by the better stories both in Stevenson's output and in the art of the short story.

IV

What do we demand of a short story before we are willing to consider that it deserves the name of art? And is art, as I am sorry to know that many admirers of Stevenson would at this juncture ask, worth bothering about? Art is surely the quality which distinguishes some of these stories from others; and art, to me, is the disinterested rendering, to perfection, of a theme intensely felt through, and in accordance with, the artist's philosophic conception of life. I do not suggest that art must involve the conscious expression of a consistent philosophy. I think it should not do that. But unless a writer has a considerable æsthetic and emotional experience which does directly inform his work with a wisdom greater than our utilitarian scheme of conventional morality, no practical experience of life and no sense of æsthetic form can suffice to make that writer an artist. Mr. Clive Bell, in his very brilliant and amusing book "Art," says that "art is significant form," which is a very much better and less pretentious definition than the one I have given. It is also easier to apply; but I purposely added a reference to the artist's philosophic conception, because it seems to me that there can be no art which is not primarily a thing of unblemished artistic sincerity. A thing pretended (artistically, not morally pretended) can, I think, no more be art, in spite of its significant form, than it can be artistically sincere. It may be retorted that there is nothing in this connection between the artist and the charlatan; but there is. There is the craftsman, one who, denied or forgoing the artist's intellectual basis, makes goods like unto works of art, which are charged with significance of form, but not with that consistency with philosophic belief which makes significant the artistic vision. For the artist's vision is not merely executive: it is conceptual. And while significant form means perfect execution of the artist's concept, there must be a relative connection between the concept and the artist's fundamental, and possibly inscrutable or inexpressible, "idea." Otherwise the brilliant men would have it all their own way, which is obviously not the law of such things. To take an example. I regard *The Pavilion on the Links* as doubtful art. In form it is better than certain stories which seem to me superior in content, better than, say, *The Beach of Falesá.* But it seems to me empty, without heart, so that its warmth is like the warmth of anger, and is chilled when its excitement is done. Ought there not to remain in one's mind, when the story is finished, some other emotion than stale excitement? I think there ought. I think that an æsthetic emotion remains in the case of all art that is really art; that one continues to feel, not the immediate clash of will or incident, but the author's true emotion, of which the mere incidents of the story are only the bridge which the author has chosen to bear his emotion by symbol, or example, into our hearts. If I were to say of *The Pavilion on the Links*: "It is not *true*," I should by ninety-nine of every hundred people be called unimaginative, and told that "nobody ever said it was." But of course I should mean, not that the incidents were rare, but that Stevenson had never *artistically* believed them, that they hung suspended in the air only by virtue of their power to interest or to excite, by means of the "heat of composition." I should mean that Stevenson had not first *imagined* the story, but that he had planned it in cold blood, saying, "We'll have an estate, and a pavilion, and two men who have quarrelled . . ." and so on, when he might equally well have been planning to describe a dairy, or a balloon, or a cataclysm at St. Malo. If I look for emotion in the story I find none. If I look for an æsthetic idea I find none. Perhaps that is where Mr. Bell revives. The story stands there as a piece of virtuosity; and if that is deliberate virtuosity, if there is no artistic conviction behind it, then the story is a fake. I think it is a fake. I am quite ready to think of it as an extraordinary clever piece of business. But if it is fake, it is not art. Does significant form imply the presence of a conviction or merely of craft?

On the other hand, I find what I should like

to call conceptual integrity in *Thrawn Janet* and in *The Beach of Falesá*, and these stories seem to me to be art. For the same reason, *The Treasure of Franchard, Providence and the Guitar*, and *The Bottle Imp* seem to me to be art. In all these stories I am conscious of æsthetic conviction. I am aware of that delightful emotion also in *The Young Man with the Cream Tarts*, and in other parts of *The Suicide Club*, but not in all. I see art baulked by literature in *Will o' the Mill*, in *Markheim*, and *Olalla*; and, greatly muddied by clotted moralising, in *Dr. Jekyll and Mr. Hyde*, which as a whole is suspiciously glib, as though it had been falsified in the transformation from dream to morality. I do not find art in the other short stories by Stevenson. They seem all to have been produced, some from one impulse, some from another, some with painstaking shrewdness, some from vanity, some even from a want of something better to do. The artist receives an inspiration, which shapes his work with the fine glow of vitality (much as a sick person is transformed by mountain air, until his features shape and colour into a new fleshly verve). The craftsman waits upon invention, and sedulously cultivates its friendliness, with a thrifty economy which brings him in the course of his life much respect from his fellows. *Dr.*

Jekyll and Mr. Hyde was dreamed by an artist; and was written by a craftsman. If Sir J. M. Barrie had, as Stevenson once wrote, "a journalist at his elbow," shall we not admit that, in the same position, Stevenson had an equally dangerous devil, who goes by the name of a craftsman?

V

If what has been said above has any applicability to this matter, we have reduced to five the number of Stevenson's short stories to which we can give the name of art. In mentioning that number, I have ventured to eliminate *The Suicide Club*, which contains several episodes, excluding *The Young Man with the Cream Tarts* whose particular character does not seem to me to warrant the use of the term "art." That leaves us with *Thrawn Janet*, *The Beach of Falesá*, *The Bottle Imp*, *Providence and the Guitar*, and *The Treasure of Franchard*. One of these is a "bogle" story, one is a realistic story of adventure in the South Seas, one is a fairy tale, and the others are light comedies, touched with fancy which transfigures without falsifying the underlying artistic sincerity of their conception. We have eliminated, for what may in some cases appear to be insufficient reasons, some twenty odd stories (counting the various episodes of *The Rajah's Diamond* and *The Dynamiter* as stories). Of the whole number of stories, two (or, with the little tale in *Catriona*, three) are concerned with "bogles," namely *Thrawn Janet* and *The Body-Snatcher*. Two others are also concerned with the supernatural: they are *The Bottle Imp* and *The Isle of Voices*. Three are psychological—*Will o' the Mill*, *Markheim*, and *Olalla*. Four are light comedies—*The Story of a Lie*, *John Nicholson*, *The Treasure of Franchard*, *Providence and the Guitar*. Two are picturesque or romantic tales of incident—*The Pavilion on the Links* and *The Merry Men*. One is a realistic tale of incident—*The Beach of Falesá*. The rest belong to a class of fantastic mystery or criminal tale which is not, apart from the attractiveness of its mayonnaise, intrinsically of great value. It is from the five tales named at the beginning of this section that we shall perhaps draw our best material for the appraisement of Stevenson's chief success as a short-story writer.

Thrawn Janet, then, is an extraordinarily successful tale of the devil's entry into the body of an old woman, imagined with great power, and told with enormous spirit. *The Beach of Falesá* is the narrative, by a trader, of his arrival at a South Sea island, his marriage to a native girl, and his overthrow of a treacherous rival. The character of the man who tells the story—Wiltshire—is well-sustained, the character of Uma, the native wife, is amazingly suggested, considering how little we see her and considering that we receive her, as it were, through the trader's report alone. For the rest, the story has vividness of local colouring, and a good deal of feeling. *The Bottle Imp*, the fairy tale, is told without fault in a manner of great simplicity. It relates to the successive purchases and sales, the sales always, by the conditions of purchase, being made at a figure lower than that of the purchase, of a magic bottle as potent as Aladdin's lamp ; and to the certainty of Hell which is involved in the continued possession of the bottle until the lessee's death. The story was written for the Samoan natives, and, as far as I am able to judge, it bears in a remarkable degree the impress of native ways of thought. It has, that is to say, the *naïveté* and gravity of the folk-tale. *Providence and the Guitar* is a gay story of the misadventures of some travelling musicians who receive poor welcome from those whom they seek to entertain, but who reconcile at length the claims of art and duty as they find them opposed in the lives of certain disunited hosts. *The Treasure of Franchard* is the simple tale of an eccentric philosopher, his more stolid wife, and of a little boy whose wisdom leads him to check, by means which are proved legitimate only by their adequacy, the philosopher's diversion from the path of happiness. The theft by the waif of certain treasure which the philosopher has discovered, to the risk of his immortal soul and the danger of his present happiness; and the appropriate restoration of that treasure when it will be of vital service—upon so slight an invention does the story progress.

The point to be observed in all these stories is that they possess unquestionable unity. Only one of them, *The Beach of Falesá*, is in any true sense a narrative. The others are examples of situation imposed upon character. In each there is an absolute relation between the conception or inspiration and Stevenson's treatment. Each will bear the pressure which may legitimately be exerted by the seeking imagination. In *Providence and the Guitar* alone is there the least air of accident; and for this reason *Providence and the Guitar*, which has this slight air of possible manipulation, is less good than the others. *The Beach of Falesá*, although a narrative, and although its perfection of form is thus affected (since, with our consciousness of narrative, is interrupted the singleness of our æsthetic emotion) has a strict consistency of action. Whether this consistency is native, or whether it is aided by the imagined personality of the narrator, which may thus impose an artificial unity upon the tale, I am unable to determine. The other three stories, *The Bottle Imp*, *Thrawn Janet*, and *The Treasure of Franchard*, granting to each story its own convention, seem to me to be perfect examples of their craft.

VI

To have written three such stories would alone be a sufficient performance to give Stevenson's name continued life among our most distinguished writers. That, in addition to these three stories, he should have written two others of such considerable value as *The Beach of Falesá* and *Providence and the Guitar*, and so many more of varying degrees of excellence, from *The Pavilion on the Links* and *The Suicide Club* to *The Merry Men* and *The Isle of Voices*, is, I think, enough to warrant a very confident claim that Stevenson not only was at his best in the short story, but that he was among the best English writers of short stories. His particular aptitude in this branch of his many-sided talent was due, as I have said, to the fact that he was here able to see and to perform with a single effort which did not unduly strain his physical endurance. Whereas, in continuous effort, he lost the strength of his first impulse in the exhausting labour which is involved in any lengthy exercise of the imagination, in the short story he was able to give effect immediately to his impulse to set out or to create complete his imagined or invented theme. What fluctuation there is to be observed of talent or performance is due entirely to the nature of his inspiration. If the idea came unsought, if some clear and inevitable idea for a short story suggested itself to him, the result, providing it was suited to his genius, and not merely to his literary ability, was a short story of distinguished or even of first-class quality. If, in the pursuance of his business as a literary craftsman, he "hit-on" a practicable plan for a short story, the result was almost certain to be distinguished in craftsmanship, acceptable to the wide and diversified tastes of the educated public, and, in fact, to be distinguishable from his genuine works of art only by the application of some test which should call in question the nature of his preliminary inspiration.

Stevenson was so distinguished a craftsman that he could often deceive his critics, but for that deception I do not think he can be held morally responsible. His other habit, of being able to deceive himself about the nature of his inspiration—exemplified, I believe, in *The Suicide Club*, for reasons which I have already given—is more serious. It is a habit illustrated with more force in the longer romances, and takes the form of beginning a story with a genuine romantic notion (or, if the reader prefers, inspiration), of finding that inspiration fail, and of proceeding nevertheless with the work so begun, relying upon his talent, his invention, or his literary skill to carry through the remaining performance at a level near enough to that established by his first inspiration to convince (at its worst, to delude) the reader. This habit, I am sure, was not indulged in bad faith; it was sometimes, perhaps nearly always, unconscious, or only partly conscious. It very likely is the habit of all modern writers whose work is regulated by the laws of supply and demand. Equally, it was possibly the habit of all past writers of fiction, because they too were affected in the same way. But in Stevenson's case the supply of a commodity took a peculiar form of falseness which proved much to the taste of his readers. It took the form of a sort of deliberate romanticism with which I have dealt at length in the next chapter, and to which I have given the more exactly descriptive term of picturesqueness. I believe this sort of romanticism gave rise to such a story as *The Pavilion on the Links*; and if I am right in regarding such picturesqueness as a bastard form of art, as, in fact, a particularly cunning form of craft, then its persistence in Stevenson makes all the more wonderful, and all the more notable, his magnificent performance in the stories singled out for praise in the present chapter. It also enforces the desirability of some very close discrimination between the work of Stevenson which is the genuine product of his indubitable genius and the work which was produced by his talent, his invention, and his literary skill.

VIII

NOVELS AND ROMANCES

I

In beginning this chapter upon that section of Stevenson's work which, whatever may be one's impression of its intrinsic merit, has at least the importance of being the section most considerable in bulk, I should like, as a matter of convenience, to define several terms in the sense in which they will be used in the course of the chapter. It should be clearly understood at the outset that the proposed definitions are to be given, not with any claim for their ultimate value, but as a mere precaution against misunderstanding. In each case the term is one which often is very loosely used; and it seems the most honest thing, as well perhaps as the most wary, to say very simply what one understands by such and such words. Many writers who do not define terms have the irritation of finding those terms counter-glossed by other critics acting in all good faith, and the consequence is that they seem to be made responsible for meanings divergent from those which they hold.

By the word "imagination," then, I mean that power of sympathy which enables a man to understand (i.e. to put himself in the place of) the invented figure or scene which he is describing either in words or in thought. I do not mean by the exercise of will, but by the spontaneous outflowing of full or partial perception. By "imagination" I mean nothing galvanic or actively creative; but an emotional translation, as it were, of the creator's spirit into the object created. Creation, the act of bodying forth the imaginations in form either symbolic or conventional, requires "invention." "Invention," whether of incident or of character, is what is generally meant by writers who use the word "imagination." Writers often say that work is "imaginative" because it has a sort of hectic improbability; but they mean that it exhibits a riotous or even a logical inventiveness, not that it shows any genuine power of imaginative sympathy. Invention, one may say, is essential to a work of imagination: it is the fault of much modern novel-writing that it is poor in invention, a fact which stultifies the writer's imagination and gives an unfortunate air of mediocrity to work which is essentially imaginative. The creation of an atmosphere is founded upon imagination; but in the absence of invention the modern imaginative writer too frequently bathes in atmosphere to a point of tedium, and then attempts to give vitality to his work by mere violence of incident or of language. The word "imaginative" (defined by all persons so as to include their own pet limitations) is often used by unimaginative writers in descriptions of lonely children, a fact which has led those who have been lonely in childhood to ascribe to themselves an attribute so much admired; but Stevenson, I think, has a rather good comment upon this sort of broody dullness when he describes "one October day when the rusty leaves were falling and scuttling on the boulevard, and the minds of impressionable men inclined in about an equal degree towards sadness and conviviality." That lowness of spirits which makes a man respond to external influences is well known; but to describe susceptibility or impressionability as imagination is misleading. A cat is very impressionable; but a cat's apparent intuitions in the matter of food or even of good-will are not understanding as the term has been defined. Imagination, therefore, may be said to be over-claimed, for the word is loosely used in most cases, even by practised writers, where " invention " or " fancy " would more properly fit. In particular it is the habit of all minor critics whatsoever to use the word "imagination " when they ought rather to use the term " poetic invention." It is that confusion which renders valueless so much criticism of modern fiction, in which the authors, being by tradition under no compulsion to be poetical, are frequently condemned as unimaginative because they follow the tradition of their craft.

A second distinction which it is desirable to make in view of what follows is the one between Romance and Realism. The word " romance " is used in a sort of ecstasy by too many conventional people ; the word " realism " is by such critics applied to one particular technical method. It has seemed better for the immediate purpose to restrict the word " romance " to a purely technical meaning, since Romance, to have any value whatever, must form a part of our conception of reality. It is the divorce of Romance from Reality which has led to its decay ; it is not that Romance has been cruelly done to death by Realism. Romance since Stevenson has become sentimental and unbelievable. That is why Romance has no friends, but only advocates. The word " romance," then, is in this chapter used to describe a fiction the chief interest in which is supported by varied incidents of an uncommon or obsolete nature. The word "novel" is applied to a fiction in which the chief interest is less that of incident and more the interest awakened by character and by a gradual relation of happenings probable in themselves and growing naturally out of the interplay of character. The word "realism" is used in relation to the critical interpretation of actual things. It must not be regarded as describing here an accumulation of detail or a preference for unpleasant subjects. For that use of the word one may refer to our leading critical journals *passim*. The accumulation of detail belongs to a technical method, and should be treated on its merits as part of a technical method. Realism, as the word is here used, is applied only to work in which the author's invention and imagination have been strictly disciplined by experience and judgment, and in which his direct aim has been precision rather than the attainment of broad effects. It is used consciously as a word of neither praise nor blame; though it is possible that I may exaggerate the merits of clear perception above some other qualities which I appreciate less.

II

Therefore, when I say that Stevenson progressed as a novelist and as a tale-teller from romance to realism I hope to be absolved of any wish to suit facts to a theory. The fact that he so progressed simply is there, and that should be sufficient. He progressed from *Treasure Island*, which he wrote when he was a little over thirty, to *Weir of Hermiston*, upon which he was engaged at the time of his death at the age of forty-four. There can be no question of his advance in power. *Treasure Island* is an excellent adventure-story; *Weir of Hermiston* seemed to have the makings of a considerable novel, incomparably superior to any other novel or romance ever written by Stevenson. Between the two books lie a host of experiments, from *Prince Otto* to the rather perfunctory *St. Ives*, through *Kidnapped* and *The Master of Ballantrae*, to *The Wrecker*, *Catriona*, and *The Ebb Tide*. One finds in *The Master of Ballantrae* the highest point of the romantic novels, not because as a whole it is a great book, but because it has very distinguished scenes; and thereafter follows a perceptible decline in raciness. Stevenson still had the knack, and could still make the supporters of his convention look as clumsy as ghouls, but his zest was impaired. He did now with pains what before had been the easiest part of his work. "Play in its wide sense, as the artificial induction of sensation, including all games and all arts, will, indeed, go far to keep him conscious of himself; but in the end he wearies for realities," said Stevenson in *The Day After To-morrow*. From the inexperience of real life which in 1882 led him, by means of a map and some literary inspirations, to make up a tale such as he thought he would himself have liked as a boy, he turned in later years to work more profound. His romance six years later than *Treasure Island* had, besides its adventures and its pawky narration, a moral theme; ten years later it had no theme at all, but a faint dragging sweetness due to the reintroduction of two old friends and the picture of a conventional heroine; at the end of his life he began three historical romances, none of which was ever finished, and only one of which ever proceeded beyond its first chapters. It is true that the pretty, heavily figured style was still at command; there was no cessation of skill. There never was any cessation of skill. If skill were needed Stevenson had it ever ready. "I have been found short of bread, gold or grace," says St. Ives; "I was never yet found wanting an answer." That is a point to note in Stevenson's equipment, that he was always very apt with the pen. Having turned writer in his youth, he remained a writer to the end. He could not dictate a letter but what the phrases ran in accustomed grooves, half-way to the tropes of his Covenanting manner. So it was that themes too slight, as in *Prince Otto*, and themes very complicated (as in *The Wrecker*), came readily to be embarked upon. He was not sufficiently critical of a theme, so long as it seemed superficially to offer some scope for his skill; which accounts for his abandoned fragments—e.g. *Heathercat*, *The Great North Road*, *Sophia Scarlet*, *The Young Chevalier*—and for the inequalities in even his best romances. Whatever theme he chose he could write upon it with such damnable skill that nothing truly came amiss or really stretched to the full his genuine talent. The theme, such as it was, lay to hand; there wanted nothing but his skill and the labour of composition. That, curiously enough, shadows out the occupation of the literary hack (a sad person who writes for money and only more money, and whose days are circumscribed by the need for continuous work in the field of romance); but although Stevenson claimed to write for money, "a noble deity" (see a humorous but truthful passage in the letter of

January, 1886, to Mr. Gosse), he claimed also to write for himself, and in this sense he was, to our relief, and in spite of any misdirected labours, an artist. There is, of course, much cant written and spoken about writing for money, both for and against; but the man who has no preference between the themes upon which he will write for money must be a very professional writer, and the hack is only a base virtuoso. That is why it is worth putting upon record that Stevenson, after saying he wrote, not for the public, but for money, added: "and most of all for myself, not perhaps any more noble (i.e. than money), but more intelligent and nearer home." He wrote variously from diversity of taste: a more interesting and tantalising question is that of his object.

III

Mr. Henry James, in criticising a selection of our modern novelists, describes himself as reading their work with, one imagines, continuous interest, and then, in face of all the phenomena which have industriously been gathered for his inspection, asking for something further. Mr. Henry James, apparently, wants to know "why they do it." It would not be in place here to say that the modern novelists are all to some extent followers of Mr. James; but it is very interesting to put that same question (amounting to a sort of *cui bono?*) to the romantic novelists. One would like to know what Stevenson aimed at in his romances. One does not receive from any one of the romances the thrill given by a perfect work of art. Their interest is broken and episodic; they fall apart in strange places, and show gaps, and (as in the case of works by Wilkie Collins and Mr. Conrad) one or two of them, including *The Master of Ballantrae*, are patched together by means of contributory "narratives" and "stories" which can never, whatever the skill of their interposition, preserve any appearance of vital form, and which, at the best, can be no more than exhibitions of virtuosity. They retain their continuity of interest only by means of the narrator's continuance; and the use of "narrations" itself is a device throwing into strong relief the incongruities of the tale and its invented scribe. They offend our sense of form by all sorts of changes of scene, lapses of time, discursiveness, and those other faults which are nowadays so much remarked. And, above all, once the last page is turned, we remember one or two characters and one or two incidents, and we wonder about the corollary, or whatever it is that Mr. James wonders about. We have been entertained, excited, amused, sometimes enthralled. In reading the books again, as we are soon, because of our forgetfulness, able to do, we recover something of the first pleasure. But of Stevenson's aim we can discover no more than we can discover of the aim of the hack-writer. We feel that his work is better, that it has greater skill, that it is graceful, apt, distinguished even. We feel that, of its kind, it is far superior to anything since written. Was there any aim beyond that of giving pleasure? Need we look for another? It is true that the problem-novel is discredited, and it is true that our most commercially successful novelists are those who can "tell a story." It is also true that our so-called artistic stories are like the needy knife-grinder. I propose to return later to this point, so we will take another one first. "Vital," says Stevenson, "vital—that's what I am, at first: wholly vital, with a buoyancy of life. Then lyrical, if it may be, and picturesque, always with an epic value of scenes, so that the figures remain in the mind's eye for ever."

We may well grant the picturesqueness; and we may grant a nervous buoyancy of fluctuating high spirits. Through all the novels there are passages of extreme beauty, to which we may grant the description "lyrical"; and many of the famous scenes have value which it is open to anybody to call epical if they wish to do so. It is the word "vital" that we find difficult to accept, and the "buoyancy of life." For if there is one thing to be inferred from the contrivances and the slacknesses and the other shortcomings of Stevenson's romances to which we shall gradually be able to make reference, it is that they lack vitality. They have a fine brag of words, and they have fine scenes and incidents; but where is there any one of them in which the author can sustain the pitch of imagining that will carry us on the wings of a vital romance? I am referring at this moment to this one point only. I am saying nothing about the books as pieces of literary artifice. There is not one of Stevenson's own original romances that is not made in two or three or even a hundred flights. There is not one that is not pieced together by innumerable inventions, so that it is a sort of patchwork. That is a persistent defect. It is in *Treasure Island*, it is in *The Master*, it is in *The Wrecker* and it is in *Weir*, patent to the most casual glance. And the cause of that is low vitality—his own and the book's. Not one of them, not even *Treasure Island*, not even

The Master of Ballantrae, which falls in two, has any powerful inevitability. These romances are, in fact, the romances of a sick man of tremendous nervous force, but of neither physical nor intellectual nor even imaginative energy. One may see it in the flickering of Alan Breck. Alan Breck is the most famous of all Stevenson's characters, with the possible exception of Silver: does he remain vivid all the time? He does not. He loses vitality several times in the course of *Kidnapped*; he hardly attains it in *Catriona*. There is no fault there; there is a weakness. Stevenson's romances were based upon a survival of boyish interests; they are full of fantastic whips and those clever manipulations with which writers sometimes conceal weaknesses; they have a tremendous vain Scots savour of language and retort; they have exciting, impressive, and splendidly vivid scenes. But the quality they have not is the fine careless rich quality of being vital. If we think, in reading them, that they are vital, the cause of our deception is Stevenson's skill. He disarms us by his extraordinary plausible air of telling a story. We are as helpless as boys reading *Treasure Island*. But Stevenson is always telling a story without end; and it is never really a story at all, but a series of nervous rillets making belief to be a river.

There are ingredients in the story; there is David Balfour starting out from his old home, and coming to his uncle's house, and being sent nearly to his death up the dreadful stair; and there is the kidnapping of David, and then the arrival on board of the survivor from a run-down boat, who proves to be Alan; the fight; and the march after Alan; the Appin murder; and the flight of David and Alan—all magnificently described, well invented, well imagined, but all as episodes or incidents, not as a story. Something else, some other things, all sorts of other things, might just as well have happened as those things which make the story as we know it. There is no continuous vitality even in *Kidnapped*; and yet, on that score, it is the best of the romances. It has a greater "buoyancy" (though not precisely, perhaps, the "buoyancy of life") than any of the other historical romances. It does not compare with *The Master of Ballantrae* for dignity or even for the distinction of isolated scenes; but for vitality it is superior.

IV

Why Stevenson should have adopted in so many instances the curious and unsatisfactory method, involving so much falseness, of the first person singular, with those man-traps, the things the narrator could never have known, supplied by leaves from other narratives, it is hard to understand. Defoe's method was simple and laborious; but it was pure narrative, and as far as one recollects, there was none of this making up by interpolated passages. The person of the narrator was maintained all the time. So with the picaresque romances. The narrative, used by Dickens and Wilkie Collins, does indeed offer some analogy; but never a very happy example of what is at best a broken and unbelievable stratagem. Stevenson, of course, used it in a marked way in *Dr. Jekyll and Mr. Hyde*; and in *Treasure Island* one cheerfully accepts the convention (only protesting that the Doctor's interference causes a break both irritating and, technically, unscrupulous). With the exception that the Doctor's portion is somehow brought in about the middle of the book, the way the story came to be written is not allowed to worry us after the first sentence. *Treasure Island* is not, therefore, a great offender. *Kidnapped* starts in a similarly abrupt way, and this book and *Catriona* are kept fairly closely to the convention. But in *The Master of Ballantrae* and in *The Wrecker* there are several inter-narratives which, even if in the earlier book they provide certain keys, do seriously affect the form of the story.

The disadvantage of the narrator is manifest enough. Every step outside his probable knowledge must be elaborately explained, or he will become uncomfortably superhuman; he can never be in danger which deprives him of speech or the power to write, but has often lived to a green and unromantic old age by the time his marvellous faculty for remembering things leads him to "take up the pen." ("They might easily take it in their heads to give us chase," says the Chevalier de Burke, "and had we been overtaken, *I had never written these memoirs*.") If he is the hero he risks being a prig or a braggart (in *St. Ives* he is, somehow, for all his gentility, not a gentleman); and he often succeeds in being rather a ninny, albeit a courageous ninny. It is this fact, possibly, that accounts for Mr. Stanley Weyman's "gentlemen of France" and the deplorable "heroes" of many another costume romance inspired by Stevenson's examples. If he is the good old retainer,—as is Mackellar in *The Master*—he must overcome one's distrust of his sleek literary craft. These are side issues of the main one—which is that such narratives are improbable. Their apparent virtue, which in itself is a snare, lies in the fact that they keep the reader's eye focussed upon the narrator, and seem thus to give homogeneity to a book. They enable the author to refuse detachment and to mingle with his characters, tapping them upon the arm so that the reader receives their full glance, or bidding them give some little personal exhibition for the naturalness of the book. Stevenson saw, perhaps, that such a method solved some of his difficulties. He loved ease of demeanour. He could use his Covenanting style at will, with the quaint, shrewd twists of language which do not fail to strike us impressively as we read; and he could throw off the task of creating a hero whom we should recognise as such in spite of all things, as we recognise Don Quixote or Cousin Pons or Prince Myshkin. Also, the use of the "I" probably made the tale better fun for himself. It was perhaps part of the make-belief. It avoided formality; it brought him nearer his canvas; it saved him the need of focussing the whole picture. That, constructively, was, as I have suggested earlier in another way, his prime weakness as a novelist. He could not see a book steadily and see it whole. Partly it may have been that by putting himself in the frame he made the picture a panorama—"the reader is hurried from place to place and sea to sea, and the book is less a romance than a panorama" is Stevenson's own admission in the case of *The Wrecker*—but most influentially, I think, it was that he had really not the physical strength and the physical energy to grasp a book entire, or to keep his invention and imagination at any extreme heat for any length of time. Whatever may be the case of this, however, it seems clear that the first person singular is a difficult and a tricky method to employ, abounding in risk of accident, and much inclined to make for improbability, unless the writer is content absolutely to limit the narrator's knowledge to things experienced, with details only filled out from hearsay, and unless he has superhuman powers of detachment. One is inclined to suppose that Stevenson for a considerable time fought shy of the objective male central character after his failure with Prince Otto, where the use of the first person might, indeed, have been distinctly amusing as an illuminant. At any rate, fully half of his romantic tales are personally narrated; and in only one of them, where the narrator is a real character and only partially a "combatant," does the power of detachment powerfully appear.

V

Prince Otto, of course, is only one out of the many self-portraits. He is, as it were, Stevenson's Hamlet, which is not quite as good as Shakespeare's Hamlet. He is nearer to Stevenson than David Balfour, because David Balfour is an ideal, while Prince Otto is an apology. All Stevenson's heroes, in fact, are tinged with the faint complacent self-depreciation which is capable of being made truly heroic, or merely weak, or, possessed of that "something that was scarcely pride or strength, that was perhaps only refinement," very human. But not one of these heroes is complete. All, as it were, are misty about the edges. The vigorous David Balfour falls into the self-distrust, not of a young man of strength, but of a self-engrossed student; weakness is paramount in the main character in *The Ebb Tide*; the dandiacal St. Ives is at the mercy of circumstance, waiting upon the next thing, reliant only upon Stevenson's good will, horribly unmasculine in his plans to please. Mackellar is a puritanical coward, but magnificently suggested; Loudon Dodd, and even young Archie Weir, being both very moral and, one imagines, very inexperienced in the ways of life, combine courage with weakness most pitiable. They are all feminine, brave in desperation, weak in thought. They are all related to Jack Matcham in *The Black Arrow*. Stevenson admired courage, and he possessed courage, as women admire and possess courage. He loved a brave man, and a tale of adventure, as women love these things. He did not take them for granted, but must hint and nibble at them all the time, thinking, perhaps, that he was making a portrait, but instead of that making what represents for us a tortured ideal. "I should have been a man child," says Catriona. "In my own thoughts it is so I am always; and I go on telling myself about this thing that is to befall and that. Then it comes to the place of the fighting, and it comes over me that I am only a girl at all events, and cannot hold a sword or give one good blow; and then I have to twist my story round about, so that the fighting is to stop, and yet me have the best of it, just like you and the lieutenant; and I am the boy that makes the fine speeches all through, like Mr. David Balfour." That is why *Prince Otto*, long the test of the true Stevensonian, seems to us now, increasingly, a lackadaisical gimcrack, as bloodless as a conceit, losing by its spinning as a tale all the fantastic effect it might have enjoyed as one of the *New Arabian Nights*. It has a great deal of beauty, and a good deal of perception both of character and of situation; but the beauty droops and sickens among the meshes of delicate writing, and the perception is all upon the surface of life, and, even so, abstract and without the impulse of human things.

It is the faint humour of Stevenson that makes the book seem sickly. It is that faint humour which brings so much of his heroic work sliding sand-like to our feet. For it must be realised that if one is going to be romantical one must have either no humour at all (which perhaps is an ideal state) or a strong, transfiguring humour which is capable of exuberance and monstrosity as well as of satiric depreciation. Stevenson's humour was of that almost imperceptible kind which grows in Scotland, and which has given rise to the legend that Scotsmen "joke wi' deeficulty." It was dry, it was nonsensical, it was satiric; it was the humour that depends upon tone, a delicacy of emphasis or pause. It was the humour of a sick man who had high spirits and very little morbidity. Now in *Prince Otto* there is morbidity; it is not a healthy book. It could not have been written by an active and vigorous man; and I do not think Stevenson could have written it after he went to Samoa. Its literary forbear, "Harry Richmond," although a very cumbrous and mannered work, has a trenchant vigour which keeps alive our admiration after our interest has dropped. It is elaborate and pompous ; but it has power. *Prince Otto* owes its best moments to a purely literary skit on the English traveller among foreign courts : that skit, it is true, is priceless. Apart from Sir John Crabtree, however, the book depends entirely for its charm upon its faint, almost swooning, beauty of style ; and it is indeed surprising that the book should have enjoyed among Stevenson's male worshippers so much handsome appreciation. It is so quizzical, where it is not sentimental or "conventional," that it is half the time engaged in self-consumption, which is as though one should say that it is eaten up with vanity.

VI

By Stevenson's own account, the first fifteen chapters of *Treasure Island* were written in as many days. He explains that he consciously and intentionally adopted an "easy" style. "I liked the tale myself," he says ; "it was my kind of picturesque." Well, it was the simplest kind of picturesque, a sort of real enjoyment of the thing for its own sake ; and our own enjoyment of it is of the same kind.

It is extraordinarily superior to the imitations which have followed it, for this reason if for no other, that it was the product of an enjoying imagination. It is possible to read *Treasure Island* over and over again, because it is good fun. There is a constant flow of checkered incident, there is enough simple character to stand the treasure-seekers on their legs, and the book is a book in its own right. It does not need defence or analysis; it sustains its own note, and it is as natural and jolly an adventure story as one could wish. Moreover, the observation throughout is exceedingly good, as well as unaffected. It is interesting to notice how vividly one catches a picture from such a brief passage as this (in Chap. XXVII): "As the water settled I could see him lying huddled together on the clean, bright sand in the shadow of the vessel's sides. A fish or two whipped past his body." Or again, on the following page, when Jim Hawkins has thrown overboard another of the mutineers: "He went in with a sounding plunge; the red cap came off, and remained floating on the surface; and as soon as the splash subsided I could see him and Israel lying side by side, both wavering with the tremulous movement of the water." Such slight passages really indicate an unusual quality in the book. They convey a distinct impression of the scene which one may feel trembling within one's own vision and hearing. The fact that *Treasure Island* has so clear a manner, unaffectedly setting out in simple terms incidents which have the bare convincingness of real romance, gives that book a singular position among the romances of Stevenson. The further fact that the incidents have some more coherence in themselves than incidents have in some of our author's romances serves to add to the book's effect. Something of this coherence (I except from the range of this term the doctor's sudden irruption into authorship, and the picturesque but arbitrary introduction of the castaway) may have resulted from the quickness with which the tale was written. For details of the composition of *Treasure Island*, the reader may see the essay *My First Book* in *Essays on the Art of Writing*.

The Black Arrow, written later, is a tale of the Wars of the Roses, and is a much more commonplace piece of work. It is also a less original kind of story ; for serials of a similar character have always been a feature of boys' papers, as long as boys' papers have been published. There is, indeed, a constant ebb and flow of incident, but the writing is hardly recognisable as Stevenson's, and the *dramatis personæ* are without character. It might almost, apart from the fact that the hero and heroine arrange to marry, have been written by the late G. A. Henty, who perhaps, even if he had made John Matcham really John Matcham, would have substituted for violent episodes some more continuous fable.

Next to *Treasure Island* among the historical romances comes *Kidnapped*, with its brilliant pictures and its clear, confident invention. Regarded simply as a tale of adventure, it is exciting, picturesque, vivid; it has qualities of intensity (that is to say, of imagination) which make it without question distinguished work. There are pictures of the country in Chapter XVII which are full of grace and tenderness; it has a stronger, clearer humour than we find in any of the novels until we come to those in which Mr. Osbourne collaborated the incidents are immediate in their effect. To say so much is to say little enough; it is to say what must have been said in 1886, at the time the book was published. The story, however, is incomplete without *Catriona*, and *Catriona* in particular has given rise to such a very bad novel-writing convention that it is difficult to see *The Adventures of David Balfour* (which, combined, the two stories relate) as anything but a malign influence upon the

English romantic novel, an influence which has brought it to a pitch of sterility hard to forgive. It must be said at once, however, that Stevenson was always better than his imitators, and so these stories will be found superior to their imitations. *Catriona* is manifestly uninspired work, artificial through and through, a sad sentimental anecdote bringing to chagrin the reader's admiration for *Kidnapped.* It is not that *Catriona* is unreadable ; it is very readable indeed. In fact that is the trouble about the book, that it has every sort of meretricious attraction, with so little in it that will honestly bear examination. It is palpable fake ; an obvious attempt to recapture the first fine carelessness of *Kidnapped.* For *Kidnapped* is a good book. It has vitality in it, and it has Alan Breck, who, for all that his vanity has been flattered by so many adorers, remains on the whole a fine picture of a vain, brave Scot. Also good is the picture of David's uncle, which is very dryly humorous, very shrewd, and exceptionally horrible. These two pieces of characterisation, as well as some minor ones, are enough to give bones to a book that is both readable and estimable. It would be enough, I think, to justify the suggestion that *Kidnapped* is the best Scottish historical romance since Scott, and indeed one of the best modern historical romances written in what we may for the moment call the English language.

St. Ives belongs to the same order as *Catriona*. It is accomplished and bad; a fact of which a recently published letter of Stevenson's shows that he was fully and contritely aware. Skill marks it; the fable is poor and irregular; and the narrator is exceedingly unpleasant. It is worthy of remark that Sir Arthur Quiller-Couch, who completed the book, is responsible for its most impressive and thrilling moments. Otherwise it shows the passive acceptance by Stevenson of his own bad convention, and it is fit only to be popular at the circulating libraries. It is even tedious, which is a sure passport to the suffrages of those who benefit by the circulating libraries.

The Master of Ballantrae, however, is a different affair. Here we have a story which, though it is broken and incomplete, has elements of noble beauty. It loses hold upon the reader in the middle, where there is a lapse of something like seven years; and the introduction of Secundra Dass is the ruin of the book as a work of art, although no doubt, as it supplies a new interest, it may have proved welcome to those reading for distraction. There are some few pieces of sheer greatness in the book, drawn with an economy and simplicity which separates them from the inferior portions as clearly as oil and water are separated. An instance may be found in the scene where Mr. Henry strikes the Master. It would be impossible to carry over in a quotation any hint of the effect which the next sentence, in its due context, has upon the reader :

"The Master sprang to his feet like one transfigured ; I had never seen the man so beautiful. 'A blow !' he cried. 'I would not take a blow from God Almighty !'"

In the book that moment seems in some extraordinary way to bring the scene leaping to the eye. The whole scene of the duel, and especially of its sequel, is fine. There are other scenes equally magnificent : even the climax, which is a collapse, does not blind us to the fact that we had been led, by the remarkable tension of the preceding narrative, to expect a poignantly tragical, and not merely a conventionally romantic, conclusion. But the climax throws up the weakness of the book, its rambling course, its wilful attempts to follow the wanderings of a central figure so fascinating to Mr. Mackellar (and to ourselves) as the Master, its lack of framework and true body of character. The Master is clear ; Mr. Mackellar is nicely touched ; the Chevalier de Burke is pleasantly farcical. In one scene, after the duel, Lord Durrisdeer and Mr. Henry's wife seem to catch the infection of life into which the heat of excitement has thrown the whole book; but they are truly no more than puppets, and relapse before ever they have stood upright. Even the Master sometimes is no more than a collection of traits; and if the book were not so finely dressed it would assuredly cut a poorer figure. Its magnificent passages it is impossible to forget; its defects are so numerous, and so obvious to be seized upon, that it seems hard to insist that they are present. Nevertheless, they are the defects inherent in Stevenson's romances.

VII

In three novels Stevenson collaborated with his stepson, Mr. Lloyd Osbourne. The first book, *The Wrong Box*, of which Mr. Osbourne claims to have written almost the whole, need not long detain us. Its amusingness is due to repetitions of phrase (e.g. "venal doctor," which is the best of them), farcicality of scene, and easy variety of complication; but it does not succeed in being particularly amusing, after all, so that we may leave it safely among the novels enjoyably to be read in railway trains. The other two books, *The Wrecker* and

The Ebb Tide, show much more clearly Stevenson's hand. The former touches every now and then a number of his early experiences in France; and the manipulation is elaborate, wasteful, and ill-considered. But the book is engrossing. *The Ebb Tide* is to all seeming a short story, or rather, two related short stories, since it is under sixty thousand words in length, and is simplified down to certain swiftly successive incidents in the lives of four men. Both books are the result of experience in the South Seas; both seem to show, as far as it is possible for me to judge, a closer and truer (though a less heroic) understanding of men than heretofore. In another way, it may be said that we have been shown previously romantic figures, invented upon a quite well-recognised and comprehended basis of convention, doing certain things which were all in the game. Those who prefer this type of character will possibly say that the Master and Otto and Alan Breck belong to the grand style in literature, that style which gave us Medea and Prometheus and Lear. That may be so. It may be that in those novels which we have yet to consider Stevenson threw aside the grand style, which, as far as he was concerned, was the style of make-belief, the style of figure, trope, costume, and the picturesque. But, to me, Stevenson, in putting aside this grand style, which is an artificial style if it spring not from the very heart of the writer, came at last into the field of his experience and tried to show something of the world he had actually seen. That is why, to me, these last three novels of his are intrinsically the most interesting, because they were the most truly personal and original, of all that he wrote. They are faulty, and they show still at times the glister of picturesque romance; but *Weir of Hermiston* is widely recognised as Stevenson's finest work, and the other two books have certain substantial merits which may well be dwelt upon here before we arrive at the general conclusions of this chapter.

The Wrecker, then, after a curious induction, begins with the education and the artistic career of Loudon Dodd, told with an amiable spirit, and convincing us by its sketches of various kinds of life. It then proceeds to San Francisco, where Dodd joins the famous Jim Pinkerton in wild-cat schemes. At last the story proper, or, if we may otherwise express it, the story exciting, begins with the sale of a wrecked ship "The Flying Scud." Pinkerton and his ally, drawn into excessive bidding by the thought that only hidden opium can account for their opponent's pertinacity, run the price up to fifty thousand dollars, the raising of which gravely endangers their credit in San Francisco, and at that price buy "The Flying Scud." Dodd proceeds to the wreck. Meanwhile, Pinkerton becomes bankrupt; but Dodd inherits a small fortune. The "Flying Scud" is a frost. Dodd now plays detective upon the man who has tried to buy the "Flying Scud," finds him and learns the history of the boat in its details. It has been said already (by Stevenson) that *The Wrecker* is more of a panorama than a romance, and "panorama" seems a very good description for the book. This kind of romance within other romances is written with greater purpose by Mr. Conrad, who, for all his arbitrary technical clumsinesses, convinces us more of the integrity of his narrative than Stevenson is able to do for *The Wrecker* in his elaborate explanatory epilogue. It reads as though it had been written with gusto, but with licence, as though the collaborators had not scrupled to give the tale its head. Its value to us now, however, is that it gives a good, clear, realistic picture of the life it describes. The Parisian portion is unexaggerated; the San Francisco chapters are vivid; the character of Pinkerton, broad though it is, has organic life; and the voyage in the "Norah Creina," if it has not the poignant reality of Mr. Conrad's descriptions of the sea, and, if it hardly bears comparison with them, has yet a bright excitement and rapid motion of great value.[1] Another point is, that the story was written, as *Treasure Island* was written, with simplicity and for the authors' own delight. Our delight in it partly reflects their delight. Only partly, however, for our appreciation is due also to the ease with which experience—of San Francisco and of the South Seas—is here translated before our eyes into a romance that is as engrossing as its predecessors, and that retains its hold upon us without elaboration of pretence.

The Ebb Tide, although much slighter, is more firmly handled. It is in essence an anecdote; but it is closely and penetratingly seen; its power to transport us (as it were by Herrick's imagined carpet) to the South Seas, and above all its quick unobtrusive rendering of a different moral atmosphere, combine to make it excellent work. If it is not moving (and very little of Stevenson's work is moving) it is at least exciting and convincing within its natural limitations.

It is with *Weir of Hermiston*, however, that

[1] I am not unaware that some parts of this book were written by Mr. Osbourne, and that Mr. Osbourne claims responsibility for several of the passages to which the above may seem directly to refer.

Stevenson reached the height of his powers as a realistic novelist. Excepting in the handling of Frank Innes, who might almost have been hired out among our dead writers of fiction as a professional seducer, the precision of *Weir of Hermiston*, the bite of Stevenson's continuously vigorous imagination, is extraordinary. Continuity of narrative there is not: one must not demand it. But unfailing precision of imagination, a thing of great rarity, marks almost the whole of that portion of the book which we have; and is matched by the similar precision of the character drawing. Kirstie Elliott and the elder Weir are alike in the respect that they are together, even in the small compass of this fragment, the surest pieces of character created by Stevenson. The subsequent course of the fable of *Weir of Hermiston*, as described by Sir Sidney Colvin in his admirable note to the book, is terrifying to those who admire the fragment for its intrinsic qualities; but we will not seek too curiously into plans which might well have been severely modified in the writing. Certainly the first nine chapters show very few signs of romantic falsification; and if it were not for Frank Innes, the novelists' hireling, we should be disposed to fear nothing for the future.

VIII

Earlier in this chapter the question was raised of Stevenson's object in writing his romances. If we read his *Note on Realism* we shall find that he talks of "poignancy of main design," "the beauty and significance of the whole," "the moral or the philosophical design," as though that other note to Sir Sidney Colvin was but a partial exposition of his aim. The one, possibly, was a personal claim; the essay a public profession; and public confession, we are aware, is apt to cling to the more desirable aspects of the truth. But the essay has a relevant value, because it speaks of the author's rapture at being able to muster "a dozen or a score" of those essential "facts" of which "it is the mark of the very highest order of creative art to be woven exclusively." Thereafter he admits, as most writers would admit, that any work of art loses its original force as that force is spent in execution and diverted into channels unforeseen.

Without "facts" the novel cannot be written. Obviously the good novel is the one that contains significant and primary facts (not to be perceived by all, but eventually to be acknowledged by all); while the bad novel is one that contains insignificant and secondary facts (easily recognisable by all and acceptable to none). It is very easy indeed to say that. It is more difficult to apply the test; or at least, if one reads the newspaper criticism of modern novels, one finds that there seems to exist a difficulty in application. So it is that what one writer regards as significant, another writer considers contemptible; and it is very likely that we should get little satisfaction from an elaborate analysis of Stevenson's chosen "facts." Some of these facts are of the greatest importance; some of them are useless. What we must rather urge is that Stevenson, for all his talk of design and the beauty of the whole, had never the physical energy to carry his conception through on a single plane (or, of course, upon that inequality of planes which may be dictated by the character of a book). That is why none of his novels (he said, in speaking of the difficulty of writing novels, "it is the length that kills") is on an ascending plane of interest or on a level plane of performance. He simply had not the bodily strength to support the continuous imaginative strain.

Further, it is the mark of the romantic and picturesque novelist that he is dependent upon that particular form of incident which provides a prop for his narrative. In a very crude way the writer of serial stories, who ends an instalment with some ghastly suggestion of coming crime, is a type of the picturesque novelist in this connection. Stevenson, in his historical romances, was a picturesque rather than a romantic novelist; he had an eye, an ear, a nose for an effect; effects he must have, or his book would stop, since it has rarely a sufficient impetus to cover the lapse in inventive skill. It was because they offered no effects that *The Great North Road*, and *Heathercat*, and *The Young Chevalier* dried suddenly upon his pen, dead before ever they were begun. One can see in these fragments the sign of Stevenson's weakness. He was "game" enough; but he could not make romance out of chopped hay, such as *The Young Chevalier*, with its bald, hopeless attempt to galvanise the Master into life again. It was, again, the title of *The Great North Road*, the title of *Sophia Scarlet* that ran in Stevenson's head. Titles for stories! Stories to fit such titles! Is that really the way an artist works? Perhaps it is; perhaps if they had been written, and had been good stories, we should have found them appropriate to a degree. But they were never written, save as fragments; because they never had any life. They never had any *idea*. And it is in virtue of its unifying idea and its ultimate form, not its contributive incidents or its more lively occasional properties, that a novel, as such, is a good novel.

Now the one book of Stevenson's which has an idea is the one which may be mistaken for either a tract or a shilling shocker. It is *Dr. Jekyll and Mr. Hyde.* The other books have ideas, or notions, but they have behind them no unifying idea. That is why one forgets what they are about. The idea of *Treasure Island* is " boy goes on hunt for pirate's treasure . . . doctor . . . wooden-legged boatswain," and so on. The idea for *Kidnapped* may have been " boy kidnapped . . . meets emissary of proscribed Scots . . . hides . . . Appin murder . . . flight. . . recovers property." The genesis of *The Master of Ballantrae* is given in a short paper, with those words for title, which is included in *The Art of Writing.* From this very frank account, we may see that the book began in a flush of enthusiasm for "The Phantom Ship," proceeded to an aged anecdote of resuscitation, and so, piecemeal, and by the joining together of all sorts of notions old and new, reached a conception of the Chevalier de Burke. Now this sort of invention, although it delights us by its resourcefulness and ingenuity, has no relation to the romance of life as it is lived or as it has ever been lived. It is picturesque invention pure and simple (the sort of thing that makes French fairy tales such pretty reading, and that makes them in the end so empty and so much inferior to the fairy tales of other nations); and except that men love a lie for its own sake it can have no importance. Until the lies (or facts) are co-ordinated and organised to make a whole, to support each other by the new value gained by their disciplined association, they are nothing but isolated lies or facts. It is the author's brooding imagination, which is in direct relation to, and under the influence of, his own æsthetic and emotional experience, that supplies that fusion and transfusion which makes a work of art. Perfect fusion makes a great work of art, such as we may see in the best of Turgeniev's work; imperfect fusion makes an inferior work of art. But there can be no fusion without a basic idea, a unifying idea. And that unifying idea, without which the invention and imagination of scenes remains hopelessly episodic, does not arise in Stevenson's romances. It shows faintly in *The Ebb Tide* and *The Master of Ballantrae*, where both books are tinged with suggestions of a moral idea; it shows Stevenson struggling in the grip of Jekyll and Hyde in the book which bears the name of those forces in him. The one (shall we say Mr. Hyde ?) is the tendency to moralise, to preach, which was inherited from countless Scottish ancestors; the other is the impulse to invent (an impulse which is too generally lauded by the great name of imagination). *Dr. Jekyll and Mr. Hyde*, dreamed as a shocker, and successful as a shocker, became in revision a parable, a morality. The natural Stevenson dreamed a shocker; and the scribe said, "Let us be moral!" And that is *Dr. Jekyll and Mr. Hyde* as we have it in its bald police-court narratives and letters. Nearer than a moral idea, Stevenson never approached our philosophical basis. Adventure blurred his sight; picturesqueness lured him. His object in writing was not the utterance of piercing thoughts or poignant emotion: he wrote because of his long Scots tongue, which turned and savoured all the lively incidents which his brain conjured. Excepting in *The Master of Ballantrae*, where our hearts are made to leap, and in *Weir of Hermiston*, which stands alone among all his books, are we ever moved by Stevenson's romances ? We are stirred by the sense of an open road, and the inviting hills, and furze and whin that is good cover for men crawling upon their bellies. We have the sense that a sentry is round the curve of the hill; but *never that he will discover us and strike.* There is never any real danger in Stevenson's books; never a real broken heart or a real heaven-high splendour of joy. There is the lure of the road and the heather; but we will be back again in the bright warm house, by the light of the red fire, with our cigar and whisky-and-soda (for it seems that is inevitable) before nightfall. It is true that we shall hear the sea, and the coach's winding horn, and some faint combing of the bagpipes; and perhaps we shall see the lamplighter, and have had scones for tea, and shall read Blackstone or some old Scots history before we go to bed. But we have not really been far away; we have been excited and pleased and happily warmed by the day's doings in the open air, but we have never seen the naked soul of man, or heard the haunting music of the syrens, or looked upon the open face of God. Nor have we truly exercised our energy in some less conventional rapture of the world's wonder. The reason may be traced back to our author: it is not a part of our own shortcomings. Stevenson, in his romances, played with his inventions; and he played sometimes splendidly. But he had not the vital assurance, the fierce trenchant fathoming of adventure that a vigorous man enjoys. "A certain warmth (tepid enough)," he says, "and a certain dash of the picturesque are my poor essential qualities." Well, that is a modest under-statement; but, as far as the historical romances go, the verdict is not wholly astray. It is in the latest novels, the realistic novels, that Stevenson rose to a fuller stature; that was because in the last years of life he truly for the first time was able to taste the actual air of physical danger. He had been in genuine physical danger: it electrified him. It gave him, perhaps, a philosophy that was not made up of figured casuistries. It enabled him to begin *Weir of Hermiston* with something of the cold freshness of running water.

IX

CONCLUSION

I

If, in writing such a book as this, one could truly succeed in grasping the significance of a man's work, or in appreciating the bent of his mind ; and then, having grasped or appreciated, if one could convey the results with any precision, the book would have a significance beyond that of literary criticism. Having "drawed a man," as Stevenson once did, one might indeed go on to "draw his soul," as Stevenson only offered to do. And the consequence might be that one would throw some light upon that difficult problem—the psychology of genius. For we may seek deliberately now, or, if deliberateness seem too dryasdust, we may seek intuitively, to understand the way in which such a man as Stevenson grew up to be a successful writer, and the aspects in which the art of writing appeared to at least one of its exponents. I have tried here and there in this book to indicate something of the spirit in which Stevenson approached his art, and I have tried also to suggest what I regard as the particular strengths and shortcomings of Stevenson's talent. But however one may interpret the work of a writer there must always be the danger that in pursuing an examination such as this one may be missing the very significance of which one is in search. At best, one can offer only tentatively the conclusions to be drawn from the results of such an examination.

Much has been written of Stevenson's indebtedness in early days to other writers. He has committed himself to the suggestion that he coveted the power of writing before he was aware of anything that he particularly wished to write. For the purpose of learning to write, he claims to have imitated a dozen different authors, assiduously practising until he had obtained a mastery over words. My own impression, which I have given earlier, is that Stevenson's *sense* of style was developed by the histrionic gifts of his nurse. That seems at least probable. I think that with a sense of style, a habit of spinning tales (which it appears that he possessed, in common with many people with no pretensions to literary skill), and a desire to write that was keen enough to be a hunger, Stevenson is a credible figure of youth. There must be many youths who get so far and go no further. The point about Stevenson is that he went on. But he went on as he began—as a writer, one who was determined to utilise words. Wherever he went he took the little notebook of which he has given an account; and he made the attempt to put everything he saw into words which expressed it exactly. The reader will find in early essays many curiously apt descriptions of natural phenomena—such, for example, as "the faint and choking odour of frost"—which show that when once Stevenson began to write away from the model he began also to observe consciously and to reproduce his sensations with what would nowadays be called "a photographic accuracy." I have already quoted two such accuracies from *Treasure Island*, where they are very effective; but it would be hard to stop quoting Stevenson if one wished to record apt phrases, for apt phrases are as common with Stevenson as leaves on a tree.

What the reader next proceeds to question is the matter which the writing is used to convey. Until we come to such an essay as *Ordered South*, I believe there is very little life in this matter. In *Roads* there is a little weak vanity, as of fancy paralysed by self-consciousness, such as one may often see in the work of very young writers; but there seems no doubt that, by 1874, a year after the composition of *Roads*, Stevenson had reached a degree of proficiency which, given a suitable subject, enabled him to escape the flaccidity which besets a young writer. Poverty of matter, which forces him back upon incident or upon thin moralising, is, throughout, a defect of Stevenson's writing. I suppose that the method by which he worked was too "near," too self-conscious, to allow his mind ever to become rich and fallow. He was using up his experience too immediately and too continuously as literary material for any very great richness to mature. He is never, that is to say, a rich writer: whatever compression there is in his work is the compression that comes of the excised word and the concentrated phrase rather than the pregnancy of thought, whether vigorous or abstruse. It must be remembered that, wherever he went, his journey or his place of residence provided him almost at once with a practicable background for literary work of some sort. His travel books, his stories—these all show immediately the stage of his life's journey to which they belong.

That is one thing. Another is that his

writing is very clear. It is a model in its freedom from ambiguities. If clarity is a virtue in writing, as I believe it to be, then Stevenson deserves praise for most admirable clarity. There is no difficulty of style. It is easy to read, because it has so much grace; but it is also easy to understand, because it is in a high degree explicit. It is essentially a prose style; as I think Stevenson was essentially a prose-writer. His poems have this same clearness (though surely he was never a master of poetic form to the extent to which he was a master of prose), and clearness in poetry is a less notable virtue than clearness in prose. Unless poetry expresses something that could not properly be expressed in prose it clearly has no claim upon our attention. The consequence of this is that Stevenson, who wrote very capable verses, does not impress us as a poet. Even in this respect, however, his clearness has its virtue; because the mark of the ostentatiously minor poet is obscurity of diction. Stevenson was not obscure in diction, and he was not obscure in thought, as so many writers with little to say are obscure. He went, in fact, to the other extreme. His poems are too explicit to be good poems. They are the poems of a man with all his wits about him; they are the poems of a man who always had his wits about him. I will go so far as to say that a man who always, in this common but expressive phrase, has his wits about him is never within measurable distance of being a poet.

If Stevenson's habitual attitude of mind be then examined it will prove to be directly opposed to the habit of mind of the poet. He was about as poetic as a robin. But his habit of mind (unlike that of the robin) was moral as well as practical. It was not philosophical; nor would one willingly use in this connection the word spiritual. It was moral and practical; it was fundamentally a prose habit of mind. The highest and the lowest were alike strange to Stevenson's mind; it had excellent equipoise, an admirable sanity. It had not, normally, a very wide range of sympathy or interest. I have explained this—or rather, I have tried to explain it—to some extent in earlier chapters; but in this place an explanation may be more clearly offered. Stevenson, we know, was an invalid; his vitality was poor, although the poverty of his vitality was partly concealed by a buoyancy of nervous high spirits. The tendency of all natures is to adjust the indulgence of emotion to the power of withstanding the reaction from such emotion. Highly emotional natures, unless they are morbid, seek instinctively to avoid the exhaustion which overstrained emotion produces. Delicate persons instinctively avoid mental exertion—not from lack of courage, or even from lack of intellectual strength; but purely from lassitude and the dread of lassitude. They do not essay long or vehement excursions from their base of common-sense; they must always be able to return the same night. That is because sustained imaginative effort, as well as poignant emotion, is instinctively recognised as dangerous. It is not that they lack the power to imagine or to feel deeply; it is simply that, as a measure for their own protection, they rely upon the virtues which are less intense and less exacting. They grow cautious. Stevenson was cautious. To him God was a kindly, well-intentioned person of infinite mercy; but He was not a terrible God, nor a God in Whom there was any mystery. If one had used the word "mystery" to Stevenson he would have thought inevitably of Gaboriau. I should explain that by suggesting—not that Stevenson was what is called "unimaginative," but that his delicate body provoked the compromise. Otherwise he might have been a fanatic. Perhaps I am wrong; perhaps there was simply nothing of the mystic in Stevenson, and perhaps there was nothing of the mystic in Alison Cunningham. It is true that Stevenson's early wrestlings with religious difficulties seem to have led him to conclusions strictly utilitarian, by which Christianity became a "body of doctrine" rather than a cloud of witnesses. Nevertheless, I am disposed to think that his apparent failure to apprehend any faith more exacting than a lucid morality or ethical code was caused throughout by physical weakness.

The point is interesting rather than conclusive; and it may be thought that Stevenson's attitude to his art tells strongly against my hypothesis. He was essentially technical in his attitude to style and to art in general. He did not regard writing as a means of expressing truths; he seems to have regarded it as an end in itself. He does not seem to consider the notion of writing to express an idea; his impulse is to gather together as many incidents as will make a book. It is easy, of course, to take an unsophisticated view of art, and pretend that the artist invariably works with the aid of an inner light. I do not wish to pretend that the artist is such a mere instrument; particularly as the writer who claims to be no more than a medium is generally no less than a charlatan. But I cannot help remarking how entirely absent from any declaration by Stevenson is the sense of an artist's profound disinterested imagining. So far from being profoundly disinterested, he seems to have followed here the custom he admits following in childhood, that of reading and watching everything for the sake of wrinkles subsequently to be used in play. It seems as though he took imaginative writing at its lowest valuation, as so much "fake," as so much invention very ingeniously contrived but never really, in the last resort, perfectly believed by the creator—as, in fact, something "pretended." Now Stevenson's practice, in that case, is better than his theory. Scenes in his romances, and some of his short stories in bulk, are the work of an artist who was working at the bidding of his inspiration. Stevenson did, at these times, believe as an artist in the work he was making. I can give no account of the artist's state of mind; but it is quite certain that Stevenson did not "pretend" his best work, and that no artist "pretends" his best work. An artist can distinguish between that part of his work which is the result of intense belief and that part which is agnostic. Stevenson seems not to have been so sure; for his aims, whether they are at "vitality" or at the death of the optic nerve and the adjective, suggest that he invariably adopted the attitude of the craftsman, the professional writer of novels for popular consumption. Even so, he is to be applauded for his freedom from artistic cant. If he is too intent upon rattling the bones, at least that is more candid than the habit of playing the priest.

II

From this question of Stevenson's conviction, however (the question of the inevitable as opposed to the practicable), arises a further question. I have said earlier that in the case of a work of art there is left with the reader some abiding emotion, an evocation, as it were, of emotion distinct from all incidental emotions, excitements, dreads, or anxieties aroused in the course of the book. In that pervading and prevailing emotion, it seems to me, lies the particular quality which distinguishes a work of art from a work of merely consummate craft. If I question whether such abiding emotion is evoked by the longer stories of Stevenson, I am bound to answer that these do not arouse in me any emotion greater than that of interest, the consequence of a succession of pleasant excitements. The romances as a whole have great ingenuity, many scenes to which all readers must look back with recollected enjoyment. In no case does the book reappear as a whole. The recollection is a recollection of "plums." That they are good plums does not affect the validity of the argument if once the specific test suggested above is accepted. In the case of *Weir of Hermiston* the recollection is obviously difficult, because the book is a fragment : it is, however, perfectly clear and level in performance, which leads to the supposition that *Weir*, as it stands, will actually bear whatever test is applied to it. For that reason *Weir* is truly regarded as Stevenson's masterpiece among the longer stories.

With the short stories I have already dealt in considerable detail; to the remaining creative works there is no need to refer on these grounds, for the plays are admittedly poor. And indeed, I should not have raised the question about the romances if it had not been the case that very considerable claims have been made on behalf of the permanent value of Stevenson's work by many writers whose opinions ordinarily command respect. The truth is probably that all good novels, of whatever kind, whether modern or historical, must be based upon idea and upon character. To Stevenson, character was incidental. To Stevenson incident, picturesque or exciting, and the employment of an atmosphere, or appropriate " style," were the most important things in romance. That was perhaps the grave mistake which made his romances what they are, and which has very considerably affected the romantic novels published since Stevenson's time and written in accordance with his conventions. The use of conventional characters, easily-recognisable romantic types, has for twenty years and more been accepted by English romantic novelists as a legitimate evasion of the need for creating character. Thus it happens that so few modern romantic novels have at this time any standing. Their names are forgotten (except, possibly, by their authors, and by some sections of the public only if the novels have been made into stage plays). If Stevenson's romances had enjoyed the strength of definite themes, and if they had been based upon character, the whole position of the romantic novel in England at the present day might have been different. As it is, the romantic novel is a survival. The freshness of Stevenson's manipulated convention is stale, and the imitators of Stevenson have forsaken romance for the writing of detective mystery stories. They still have popularity ; but they have no status.

CONCLUSION

III

But it may be urged that Stevenson saved his ideas for that more direct appeal to readers which is the special privilege of the essay. Now the point in this case is to be reached by the inquiry as to what ideas Stevenson expressed in his essays. They are very simple. Stevenson's essays are either fanciful treatments of pleasant, or attractive, or ingenious notions; or they are frankly homiletic. Stevenson loved courage, and he thought that courage should have trappings. To his mind the bravest actions were the better for a bit of purple. But when we penetrate beyond this crust of happy truism there is little that will reward us for the search. There is no thought, and little enough feeling in the essays: their charm lies in the fact that they dress prettily, and sometimes beautifully, the rather obvious philosophical small-change which most people cherish as their private wisdom. The essays flatter the reader by mirroring his own mind and giving it an odd twist of grace. They are shrewd mother-wit, dressed for a fairing. That is what causes the popularity of the essays—that and the air they have of "looking on the bright side of things." They do look on the bright side; they are homely, cheerful, charming; they will continue to adorn the bookshelf with a pretty, pale, bedside cheerfulness which will delight all whose culture exceeds their originality. But I believe that they have ceased to be regarded (it has almost become ridiculous that they should ever have been regarded) as comparable with the essays of Montaigne, or Hazlitt, or Lamb; because their day is sinking and their fragility is seen already to indicate a want of robustness rather than a delicacy of perception. By this I do not mean to suggest that already the essays are out of date: they are only out of date in some instances, and even if they were completely out of date that fact would not have much ultimate critical significance. What is, however, very significant, is that they have ceased to stand as essays, and have become goods for the monger of phrases. Their "aptness," which of old was the charm that dignified the trite moralism, has recoiled upon them: they are seen to be mere aggregations of "happy thoughts," fit to be culled and calendared for suburban households. It is not without its pathos that one warning against too-eager judgment of weaker brethren, really written by an American woman poet, is widely and steadfastly attributed to Stevenson by his greatest admirers. For the teaching of the essays is one of compromise, not of enlarged ideals; it is the doctrine of "that state of life" which finally ends in a good-natured passivity not unlike the happy innocence of the domesticated cat. Thus, for all his powerful desire to preach, Stevenson taught nothing but a bland acquiescence; for the field of battle to which he likened marriage as well as life was a field in which there was no headstrong conflict of ideal and practice, but a mere accommodation which a phrase could embody.

IV

There seems to be a general tendency to protest against such opinions, not because the opinions are adequately countered, but because in most readers Stevenson produces a vague doting which is entirely uncritical. Stevenson in such warm hearts is incomparable; and a question is a perceptible rebuff to their confidingness. The prevailing feeling appears to be one of affectionate admiration, a matter of personal attraction rather than of critical esteem. Such a claim in any man is very far from being negligible. It is clear that the need of most people is an object of affection. They must love, or they cannot appreciate. The modern school of novelists, which tries to be very stern and almost legally unjust, provides little enough material for the loving hearts. The modern school says to its readers: "You are wicked, selfish, diseased, but horribly fascinating, and I'm going to set you right by diagnosis"; and the reader feels a sting in the fascination. Stevenson says, "We are all mighty fine fellows; and life is a field of battle; but it is better to be a fool than to be dead; and the true success is to labour"; and the reader feels that Stevenson is One of Us! He is not, that is to say, austere; he does not ask uncomfortable questions; he makes no claim upon his readers' judgment, but only upon their self-esteem and their gratified assent. He even tells them about himself. He says, "I knew a little boy"; and his readers say: "It's himself!" They read with enormous satisfaction.

Well, all that is delightful; but in its way it is a red-herring. It does not help us to assay the literary value of Stevenson's work. It is simply a wide illustration of the fascination which Stevenson had for his friends. It is an extension of that rare thing, personal charm. We may say that it ought not to influence readers; and no doubt it influences some too-critical readers adversely (criticism being understood by all admirers of Stevenson as the merest corrosion); but the fact is that it cannot be ignored by anyone who seeks to account for Stevenson's continued, and even now barely declining, popularity. Another very good reason is that Stevenson had extraordinarily good friends. I think it probable that no writer ever had friends more loyal and affectionate. They criticised his work privately to its great improvement, and then sold his work when it was completed, acting as counsellors and agents. And this was done with the same affectionate admiration which readers of his work still feel. He had few intimate friends, says Mrs. Stevenson: if friendship consisted in affection received (as distinguished from affection exchanged), I think Stevenson would have been in friends the richest man of his own generation. And since his death he has found a hundred thousand friends for every one he had during his lifetime. No man was ever richer in well-wishers. If he had few intimate friends that was because he was naturally reserved, or, as Mrs. Strong says, "secretive." No doubt it was a part of his charm that his friends were mystified by his reserve: I do not see why his readers also should be mystified, for his writing is free of any mystery. I can only assume that a slight air of sentimentalism which runs through essays and romances alike, and over into such short stories as *Will o' the Mill* and *Markheim*, combines with the thin optimism of the essays and the picturesque variety of incident of the romances to give body to this charm. I have stated in an earlier chapter the features of the romances which seem to me to be merits: it is not necessary to repeat the merits here. They include occasional pieces of distinguished imagination, a frequent exuberance of fancy, and a great freshness of incident which conceals lack of central or unifying idea and poverty of imagined character. Intrinsically, although their literary quality is much higher, the romances—with the possible exception of *Kidnapped*—are inferior to the work of Captain Marryat.

V

Finally, the fact which all must recognise in connection with Stevenson's work is the versatility of talent which is displayed. From essays personal to essays critical; from short-stories picturesque to short-stories metaphysical, and stories of bogles to fairy stories of princes and magic bottles and wondrous enchanted isles; from tales of treasure to the politics of a principality, from Scottish history to tales of the South Seas; from travel books to poems for men and children; from the thermal influences of forests to a defence of a Roman Catholic hero-priest; from Samoan politics to the story of the Justice Clerk; from plays to topographical history and imaginary war-news and the cutting of wood-blocks (to the satisfaction of Mr. Joseph Pennell)—that is a dazzling record. Quite obviously one cannot contemplate it without great admiration. When it is remembered also that it is the product of a man who was very frequently (though not, as is generally supposed, continuously) an invalid, the amount of it, and the variety, seems to be impossible. Yet it is possible, and this fact it is which finally explains our attitude to Stevenson. We think it marvellous that he should have been able to write at all, forgetting, as we do, that "writing his best was very life to him." We do forget that; we ought not to forget it. We ought not to forget that Stevenson was a writer. He meant to be a writer, and a writer he became. He is known chiefly in these days as a writer; and in the future he will be still more clearly seen as a writer. The weaknesses of his work will be realised; to some extent his writing will fall in popular esteem; but he will be less the brave soul travelling hopefully and labouring to arrive, and more the deliberate writer. When other men sing and walk and talk and play chess and loiter, Stevenson wrote. In his life there is no question that he sang and walked and loitered and talked and played chess; but when he could do none of these things he could write. Writing was as the breath of his body; writing was his health, his friends, his romance. He will go down into literary history as the man who became a professional writer, who cared greatly about the form and forms of expression. The fact that he concentrated upon expression left his mind to some extent undeveloped, so that he could express very excellently perceptions more suitable to his youth than to his maturer years. It made his earlier writing too scented and velvet-coated. But it enabled him, when his feeling was aroused, as it only could have been in the last years of his life, to write at great speed, with great clearness, an account of the political troubles in Samoa and in particular of German diplomacy there, which seems to us still valuable—not because the facts it records are of extreme significance, but because at the end of his life Stevenson was at last to be found basing his work upon principles, really and consciously grasped, from which the incidental outcome was of less importance than the main realisation. Where he had hitherto been shuttlecocked by his impulses, and tethered by his moralism, he became capable of appreciating ideas as of more importance than their expression. If he had been less prolific, less versatile, less of a virtuoso, Stevenson might have been a greater man. He would have been less popular. He would have been less generally admired and loved. But with all his writing he took the road of least resistance, the road of limited horizons; because with all his desire for romance, his desire for the splendour of the great life of action, he was by physical delicacy made intellectually timid and spiritually cautious. He was obliged to take care of himself, to be home at night, to allow himself to be looked after. Was not that the greatest misfortune that could have befallen him? Is the work that is produced by nervous reaction from prudence ever likely to enjoy an air of real vitality? In the versatility of Stevenson we may observe his restlessness, the nervous fluttering of the mind which has no physical health to nourish it. In that, at least, and the charming and not at all objectionable inclination to pose. He was a poseur because if he had not pretended he would have died. It was absolutely essential to him that he should pose and that he should write, just as it was essential that he should be flattered and anxiously guarded from chill and harm. But it was necessary for the same reason, lest the feeble flame should perish and the eager flicker of nervous exuberance be extinguished. That Stevenson was deliberately brave in being cheerful and fanciful I do not for one moment believe ; I think such a notion is the result of pure ignorance of nervous persons and their manifestations. But that Stevenson, beneath all his vanity, realised his own disabilities, seems to me to be certain and pathetic. That is what makes so much of the extravagant nonsense written and thought about Stevenson since his death as horrible to contemplate as would be any dance of ghouls. The authors of all this posthumous gloating over Stevenson's illnesses have been concerned to make him a horribly piteous figure, to harrow us in order that we should pity. How much more is Stevenson to be pitied for his self-constituted apostles ! We shall do ill to pity Stevenson, because pity is the obverse of envy, and is as much a vice. Let us rather praise Stevenson for his real determination and for that work of his which we can approve as well as love. To love uncritically is to love ill. To discriminate with mercy is very humbly to justify one's privilege as a reader.

CONCLUSION

VI

It is sufficient here to maintain that Stevenson's literary reputation, as distinct from the humanitarian aspect of his fortitude, is seriously impaired. It is no longer possible for a serious critic to place him among the great writers, because in no department of letters—excepting the boy's book and the short-story—has he written work of first-class importance. His plays, his poems, his essays, his romances—all are seen nowadays to be consumptive. What remains to us, apart from a fragment, a handful of tales, and two boy's books (for *Kidnapped*, although finely romantic, was addressed to boys, and still appeals to the boy in us) is a series of fine scenes—what I have called "plums"—and the charm of Stevenson's personality. Charm as an adjunct is very well; charm as an asset is of less significance. We find that Stevenson, reviving the never-very-prosperous romance of England, created a school which has brought romance to be the sweepings of an old costume-chest. I am afraid we must admit that Stevenson has become admittedly a writer of the second class, because his ideals have been superseded by other ideals and shown to be the ideals of a day, a season, and not the ideals of an age. In fact, we may even question whether his ideals were those of a day, whether they were not merely treated by everybody as so much pastime; whether the revival of the pernicious notion that literature is only a pastime is not due to his influence. We may question whether Stevenson did not make the novel a toy when George Eliot had finished making it a treatise. If that charge could be upheld, I am afraid we should have another deluge of critical articles upon Stevenson, written as blindly as the old deluge, but this time denouncing him as a positive hindrance in the way of the novel's progress. However that may be, Stevenson seems very decidedly to have betrayed the romantics by inducing them to enter a *cul-de-sac*; for romantic literature in England at the present time seems to show no inner light, but only a suspicious phosphorescence. And that fact we may quite clearly trace back to Stevenson, who galvanised romance into life after Charles Reade had volubly betrayed it to the over-zealous compositor.

Stevenson, that is to say, was not an innovator. We can find his originals in Wilkie Collins, in Scott, in Mayne Reid, in Montaigne, Hazlitt, Defoe, Sterne, and in many others. No need for him to admit it: the fact is patent. "It is the grown people who make the nursery stories; all the children do, is jealously to preserve the text." That is what Stevenson was doing; that is what Stevenson's imitators have been doing ever since. And if romance rests upon no better base than this, if romance is to be conventional in a double sense, if it spring not from a personal vision of life, but is only a tedious virtuosity, a pretence, a conscious toy, romance as an art is dead. The art was jaded when Reade finished his vociferous carpet-beating; but it was not dead. And if it is dead, Stevenson killed it.

BIBLIOGRAPHY

BIBLIOGRAPHY

(The dates within brackets are those of composition or of first periodical publication.)

The Pentland Rising, **1866.**

A New Form of Intermittent Light, **1871.**

The Thermal Influence of Forests, **1873.**

An Appeal to the Clergy of the Church of Scotland, **1875.**

An Inland Voyage, **1878.**

Edinburgh : Picturesque Notes, **1879.**

Travels with a Donkey, **1879.**

Virginibus Puerisque, **1881.**

Virginibus Puerisque : four parts (1876–1879) ; Crabbed Age and Youth (1878) ; An Apology for Idlers (1877) ; Ordered South (1874) ; Æs Triplex (1878) ; El Dorado (1878) ; The English Admirals (1878) ; Some Portraits by Raeburn ; Child's Play (1878) ; Walking Tours (1876) ; Pan's Pipes (1878) ; A Plea for Gas Lamps (1878).

Familiar Studies of Men and Books, **1882.**

Victor Hugo's Romances (1874) ; Some Aspects of Robert Burns (1879) ; Walt Whitman (1878) ; Henry David Thoreau (1880) ; Yoshida Torajiro (1880) ; François Villon (1877) ; Charles of Orleans (1876) ; Samuel Pepys (1881) ; John Knox, and his Relations to Women (1875).

New Arabian Nights, **1882.**

The Suicide Club and the Rajah's Diamond (1878) ; The Pavilion on the Links (1880) ; A Lodging for the Night (1877) ; The Sire de Malétroit's Door (1878) ; Providence and the Guitar (1878).

The Silverado Squatters, **1883.**

R. L. STEVENSON

Treasure Island, 1883.

Prince Otto, 1885.

A Child's Garden of Verses, 1885.

The Dynamiter, 1885.

Dr. Jekyll and Mr. Hyde, 1886.

Kidnapped, 1886.

The Merry Men, 1887.

The Merry Men (1882); Will o' the Mill (1878); Markheim (1885); Thrawn Janet (1881); Olalla (1885); The Treasure of Franchard (1883).

Memories and Portraits, 1887.

The Foreigner at Home (1882); Some College Memories (1886); Old Mortality (1884); A College Magazine; An Old Scotch Gardener (1871); Pastoral (1887); The Manse (1887); Memoirs of an Islet; Thomas Stevenson (1887); Talk and Talkers (1882); The Character of Dogs (1883); "A Penny Plain and Twopence Coloured" (1884); A Gossip on A Novel of Dumas's; A Gossip on Romance (1882); A Humble Remonstrance (1884).

Underwoods, 1887.

Memoir of Fleeming Jenkin (in "Papers Literary, Scientific, etc.," by Fleeming Jenkin), 1887.

The Black Arrow, 1888.

The Master of Ballantrae, 1889.

The Wrong Box, 1889.

Father Damien, 1890.

Ballads, 1890.

Across the Plains, 1892.

Across the Plains (1883); The Old Pacific Capital (1880); Fontainebleau (1884); Epilogue to "An Inland Voyage" (1888); The Coast of Fife (1888); The Education of an Engineer (1888); The Lantern Bearers (1888); A Chapter on Dreams (1888); Beggars (1888); Letter to a Young Gentleman (1888); Pulvis et Umbra (1888); A Christmas Sermon (1888).

BIBLIOGRAPHY

***The Wrecker*, 1892.**

***A Footnote to History*, 1892.**

***Three Plays*, 1892.**

Deacon Brodie (1880); Beau Austin (1884); Admiral Guinea (1884).

***Island Nights Entertainments*, 1893.**

The Beach of Falesá (1892); The Bottle Imp (1891); The Isle of Voices (1893).

***Catriona*, 1893.**

***The Ebb Tide*, 1894.**

***Vailima Letters*, 1895.**

[*Dr. Jekyll and Mr. Hyde and*] *Fables*, 1896.

***Weir of Hermiston*, 1896.**

***Songs of Travel*, 1896.**

***A Mountain Town in France*, 1896.**

***Four Plays*, 1896.**

Deacon Brodie; Beau Austin; Admiral Guinea; Macaire (1885).

***St. Ives*, 1898.**

***Letters to His Family and Friends*, 1899.**

***In the South Seas*, 1900.**

***The Pocket R. L. S.* (containing "Prayers"), 1902.**

***Essays in the Art of Writing*, 1905.**

On Some Technical Elements of Style in Literature (1885); The Morality of the Profession of Letters (1881); Books which have Influenced Me (1887); A Note on Realism (1883); My First Book: Treasure Island (1894); The Genesis of "The Master of Ballantrae" (1890); Preface to "The Master of Ballantrae" (1889).

***Tales and Fantasies*, 1905.**

The Misadventures of John Nicholson (1887); The Body-Snatcher (1884); The Story of a Lie (1879).

R. L. STEVENSON

***Essays of Travel*, 1905.**

The Amateur Emigrant (1879); Cockermouth and Keswick (1871); An Autumn Effect (1875); A Winter's Walk (1876); Forest Notes (1875–6); A Mountain Town in France (1879); Rosa quo Locorum (1890); The Ideal House; Davos in Winter (1881); Health and Mountains (1881); Alpine Diversions (1881); The Stimulation of the Alps (1881); Roads (1873); On the Enjoyment of Unpleasant Places (1874).

***Poems*, 1906.**

Underwoods; Ballads; Songs of Travel.

***Lay Morals and Other Papers*, 1911.**

Lay Morals (1879); Father Damien (1890); The Pentland Rising (1866); The Day after To-morrow (1887); [College Papers] Edinburgh Students in 1824 (1871); The Modern Student considered generally (1871); Debating Societies (1871) The Philosophy of Umbrellas (1871); The Philosophy of Nomenclature (1871); [Criticisms] Lord Lytton's "Fables in Song" (1874); Salvini's Macbeth (1876); Bagster's "Pilgrim's Progress" (1882); [Sketches] The Satirist (? 1870); Nuits Blanches (? 1870); The Wreath of Immortelles (? 1870); Nurses (1870); A Character (? 1870); The Great North Road (1895); The Young Chevalier (1892); Heathercat (1894).

***Records of a Family of Engineers*, 1912.**

***Poems*, 1913.**

Underwoods; Ballads; Songs of Travel; A Child's Garden.

The Edinburgh Edition of the Works.		27 vols.	1894–97.
The Pentland Edition	,,	20 vols.	1906–07.
The Swanston Edition	,,	25 vols.	1911–12.